The Louisiana
Legislative
Black Caucus

The Louisiana Legislative Black Caucus

Race and Representation in the Pelican State

Jas M. Sullivan and Jonathan Winburn

Foreword by Yvonne Dorsey

Louisiana State University Press
Baton Rouge

Published by Louisiana State University Press
Copyright © 2011 by Louisiana State University Press
All rights reserved
Manufactured in the United States of America
FIRST PRINTING

DESIGNER: *Mandy McDonald Scallan*
TYPEFACE: *Minion Pro*
PRINTER: *McNaughton & Gunn, Inc.*
BINDER: *Acme Bookbinding, Inc.*

All charts and other figures were drawn by Mary Lee Eggart.

Library of Congress Cataloging-in-Publication Data

Sullivan, Jas M.
  The Louisiana legislative Black caucus : race and representation in the Pelican State / Jas M. Sullivan and Jonathan Winburn ; foreword by Yvonne Dorsey.
     p. cm.
  Includes bibliographical references and index.
  ISBN 978-0-8071-4036-9 (cloth : alk. paper) — ISBN 978-0-8071-4037-6 (pdf) — ISBN 978-0-8071-4038-3 (epub) — ISBN 978-0-8071-4039-0 (mobi)
  1. Louisiana. Legislature—Caucuses. 2. African American legislators—Louisiana. 3. African Americans—Louisiana—Politics and government. 4. Louisiana—Politics and government—1951– I. Winburn, Jonathan, 1977– II. Title.
  JK4768.S85 2011
  328.763'076—dc22

2011016043

The paper in this book meets the guidelines for permanence and durability of the Committee on Production Guidelines for Book Longevity of the Council on Library Resources. ∞

For
My wife and son
Samaah and Malik
because of their love, patience, and support
   —J.M.S.

For
My girls: Amanda, Addison, and Julia
   —J.C.W.

Contents

Foreword, *by Yvonne Dorsey* xi
Acknowledgments xiii

Introduction 1
1. Black Electoral Politics 7
2. An Overview of Black Caucus History 29
3. Views from the Louisiana Legislative Black Caucus 45
4. Setting the Agenda 70
5. Turning Black-Interest Agendas into Policy 88
6. Voting Cohesion, Ideology, and Coalitions 109
Conclusion 130

Appendix: Policy Coding 141
Notes 145
Selected Bibliography 161
Index 173

Figures and Tables

Figures

2.1. States with Legislative Black Caucuses   38
3.1. Louisiana Legislators by Party, 1980–2004   48
3.2. Louisiana Legislators by Gender, 1980–2004   48
3.3. Louisiana Legislators by Race, 1980–2004   49
3.4. Louisiana Legislators by Education Level, 1980–2004   49
3.5. Louisiana Legislators' Self-Perceptions of Racial Identity   56
3.6. Representational Focus of LLBC Members   59
3.7. Representational Style of LLBC Members   59
5.1. Predicted Probabilities for Bill Passage by Group   100
5.2. Predicted Probabilities for Bill Passage by LLBC and New Orleans Delegations   101
6.1. Roll-Call Voting by Group in the House, 2005 and 2006   118
6.2. Roll-Call Voting by Group in the Senate, 2005 and 2006   119
6.3. Roll-Call Voting and Constituency Influence in the House, 2005 and 2006   120
6.4. Roll-Call Voting and Constituency Influence in the Senate, 2005 and 2006   121
6.5. Voting Coalitions in the House, 2005 and 2006   122
6.6. Voting Coalitions in the Senate, 2005 and 2006   123

Tables

3.1. Committee Leadership of Black Members in the Louisiana House and Senate, 2005–2006   51
3.2. Policy Attitudes among Black Legislators in the Louisiana Legislature, 2005–2006   53

3.3. Average Favorability of Black Leaders among Black Legislators   54
3.4. Research on the Effects of Black Racial Identity on Policy Preferences   55
4.1. Top Five Policy Areas of Legislation Introduced, by Group   71
4.2. Likelihood of Introducing Black-Interest or Race-Specific Legislation   75
4.3. Predicted Number of Black-Interest and Race-Specific Bills Introduced, 2006   77
4.4. Correlation between District Characteristics and Black-Interest and Race-Specific Agendas, 2005 and 2006   80
4.5. Personal Characteristics and Black-Interest and Race-Specific Agendas, 2005 and 2006   82
4.6. Influences on Bill Cosponsorship   85
5.1. Legislation Passage Rates for Groups' Top Five Policy Areas   92
5.2. Legislation Passage Rates by Group and Type of Legislation   93
5.3. Estimates of Bill Passage   98
5.4. Estimates for a Bill Dying in Committee   104
5.5. The LLBC Agenda and Bill Outcomes   106
6.1. Average Cohesion by Caucus or Group   113
6.2. Individual Membership Cohesion, House   114
6.3. Individual Membership Cohesion, Senate   115
6.4. Voting Coalitions   125
6.5. Winning Policy Support, 2005 and 2006   127

Foreword

As a member of the Louisiana Legislative Black Caucus for sixteen years, I have personally experienced the ebb and flow of the political battle in both Louisiana's house and its senate. Therefore, I looked forward to reading this book with considerable interest and perhaps a bit of skepticism. Would they get it right? I am pleased to say that indeed they got it more than right.

This book provides original research that will prove eye-opening for anyone interested in the issues of minority representation. You will find trends and issues illuminated here that are sometimes obscure even to the participants, distracted as we can be by the cluttering details and passions in the trenches.

Louisiana politics has a decidedly rough-and-tumble, populist bent. One unfortunate side effect is that there are precious few true statesmen and stateswomen in the state legislature; they are as out of place here as deer in a den of tigers. This may also be why our state's political consultants, like James Carville, Raymond Strother, and others weaned on Louisiana's predatory politics, occasionally emerge to devour the national sheep. Let this serve as a reminder why anyone interested in the democratic process may find a deeper understanding of Louisiana politics to be of considerable practical value.

At present, all members of the Louisiana Legislative Black Caucus come from districts in which minorities constitute the majority of voters. There is a reason for this: neither political party has ever thrown its financial or organizational support behind an African American candidate in any political jurisdiction in which a white candidate had the least chance of winning. Not once. Blacks and whites may work together, but we are segregated after five o'clock and on Sundays. Racism is surreal in Louisiana. It is important to understand, too, that many of the ways in which we carry out our mission are unsung, found in the hundreds of insidiously racially biased and one-sided bills we defeat.

Yet all of us in the Black Caucus recognize another serious responsibility: we are the sole representatives of Louisiana's poor population. Yes, the majority of Louisiana blacks, 80 percent or more, are poor, but many, many whites also suffer in poverty. These whites are seriously underrepresented; whites on welfare are not the ones being elected. Recently, a desperately impoverished majority-black district elected a new white senator and then watched as his first act was a whirlwind of legislative legerdemain to get them . . . a million-dollar golf course. What a conundrum for the citizens: a bag of rice or a bag of golf balls? Which should they use their few dollars to buy? Unfortunately, this is not an isolated instance. It has become the norm. The Black Caucus, as part of our mission, undertakes to implement and promote policies that allow *all* citizens ready access to education and economic advancement. We do not distinguish between one poor person and another in our mission statement or in our actions.

There is a deep cultural divide in the manner in which black and white constituents approach their political leaders and the types of problems they believe are appropriate for them to solve at particular political levels. These differences often puzzle and confuse our white colleagues, who frequently come to members of the Black Caucus for help and instruction on how to handle various problems brought to them by their black constituents. In this sense, we few are responsible for representing virtually all black voters throughout Louisiana.

Unfortunately, Louisiana can never erase its history. However, the members of the Black Caucus know that we must face that past honestly, learn from it, and work hard to minimize current manifestations of racial distrust. In such efforts, we strive to ensure the fair and equal treatment of all Louisianians under state law.

In this book you will find hard numbers and careful analyses that demonstrate how difficult this task has been. You may also find the inspiration to join us.

Yvonne Dorsey
Louisiana State Senator

Acknowledgments

We are grateful to the many people who have guided, supported, and encouraged us on this project. When Jas Sullivan first went to Louisiana State University, he taught a course titled "Blacks and the American Political System." The then speaker pro tempore of the Louisiana house, Yvonne Dorsey (now a state senator), was in the class. After a discussion about Sullivan's research interests, Speaker Dorsey commented, "If your research interests are on the experiences of black legislators, I will do all I can to help." That conversation and her kindness set this project in motion. Without her help, writing this book would have been very difficult. No words can adequately express our gratitude to her. We would also like to thank the many people on her staff, as well as her contacts in the community who helped with this project: Joseph A. Delpit, Randy K. Haynie, Kenyatta Morris, Patsy Parker, and Patrick Wallace. We are also indebted to the members of the Louisiana Legislative Black Caucus (LLBC) who agreed to be interviewed. The information we gained in those interviews gave us a richer understanding about their everyday legislative experiences and provided a context for understanding our empirical findings. Additionally, the LLBC staff was instrumental in providing much-needed information regarding the caucus's history, past and current members, and other resources. Lastly, we would like to thank the staff at the LSU Press for their extraordinary support and assistance throughout the publishing process.

∼

I am grateful for the support of the Louisiana State University community—administration, faculty, students, and staff. I especially would like to thank my colleagues in the Department of Political Science and the African and African American Studies Program for their support. The following individuals played an especially important role: Keena Arbuthnot, Kate Bratton, Angeletta Gourdine, Linda Smith Griffin, Wayne Parent, Meghan Sanders, and Jim Stoner. In addition, several of my graduate and undergraduate assistants made important contributions: Alexandra Ghara, Abigail Omojola, and Jessica Self.

I would also like to thank my family, friends, and academic mentors for their support and encouragement. There is not enough space here to list everyone, but I do want to recognize the following individuals because they have played such an influential role in my academic and personal life: Marijke Breuning, Larry Hanks, Marjorie Hershey, and John Ishiyama. I am especially thankful for the compassion and love my parents have shown me throughout my life.

Jas Sullivan

The University of Mississippi provided generous support for this project. This included grants from the Office of Research and Sponsored Programs and the College of Liberal Arts. Within the Department of Political Science, Bridget Hester supplied invaluable research assistance with the roll-call collection. Additionally, my friends and colleagues Bob Brown, John Bruce, Jake Kathman, and Tim Nordstrom provided the excellent work environment needed to complete this project. The institutional analysis within this book would not have been possible without the knowledge and skills learned from working with the Representation in America's Legislatures crew: Jennifer Hayes Clark, Tracy Osborn, and Jerry Wright. Finally, as always, my family deserves the most credit for supporting and putting up with me throughout the process.

Jonathan Winburn

Introduction

Questions of representation—that is, how to ensure that all people, both majorities and minorities, are fairly represented—are critical in any democracy, and issues of minority representation, in particular, are central to understanding many of these questions. An especially crucial issue in research on representation deals with the ability of minority groups to represent their constituents, who are very often minorities in the American political system. Among groups that have arisen to take on this issue are black caucuses. In this book, we take an in-depth look at the evolution and present activities of one of these groups, the Louisiana Legislative Black Caucus (LLBC), in order to help constituents better understand the effectiveness and limitations of minority legislators' representation.

The guiding theoretical framework for this study centers on two questions: (1) How do minority legislators descriptively represent their constituents beyond sharing the same race? and (2) Are minority legislators able to convert their descriptive representation to substantive representation? In addressing the first question, we explore how issues of race and racial identity influence the ways black legislators approach their jobs. We also take a look at how the backgrounds of black legislators compare with those of their constituents as well as with those of their white peers. We use this theoretical framework throughout the book to analyze the role not only of minority representatives but also of the formal caucuses they use to represent their constituents.

Without a doubt, with the move toward majority-minority districting practices in the 1980s and 1990s, American legislatures produced increases in selective descriptive representation by increasing drastically the number of black legislators. With this selection effect in place, what representational role do the black members believe they have within the legislature? We explore this important question throughout this book.

To answer the second question, we turn to policy outcomes to discern whether selective descriptive representation comes at the cost of substantive representation or whether, by means of a formal caucus, minority legislators can enhance their substantive representation while still offering the benefits of descriptive representation. In more specific terms, we ask, Are black legislators able to garner support from the white Democrats who overwhelmingly represent districts that are "cracked"[1] of a large base of the Democratic Party, black constituents, or do these white Democrats forge stronger coalitions with the Republicans?

Outline

In the first two chapters of this book, we provide a brief historical overview of the electoral struggles and successes of blacks in American politics and attempts at representing black interests over time. These chapters situate the rest of our story—which focuses on Louisiana—in a broader historical context and allow for an appropriate comparison of Louisiana to the rest of the country. We turn directly to Louisiana in the last part of chapter 2, and we focus on the state through chapter 6, returning to a broader discussion in the conclusion.

In chapter 1 we discuss the brief electoral victories during Reconstruction, the inequalities that followed until the civil rights movement of the 1960s, and the modern electoral landscape of black politicians through Barack Obama's presidential victory. We conclude with a look at some of the limits of electoral success and what these mean for issues of representation.

In chapter 2 we look at the strategies for representing black interests inside the political process. We examine the growth and development of the Congressional Black Caucus, along with the role of state legislative black caucuses across the country. We then focus the discussion on the Louisiana Legislative Black Caucus, tracing the evolution of the caucus and concluding with a discussion of the state of the modern caucus and its members.

Chapter 3 is our in-depth look at descriptive representation. In this chapter we discuss theories of representation from the viewpoint of the LLBC members based on interviews and surveys. We provide a deeper understanding of the role that minority members believe they should and do play in the state legislature. This chapter also provides an overview of Louisiana's political culture and the legislators' backgrounds, which relate to their roles of representing the black community and working with the majority white legislators.

The next three chapters move from issues of descriptive to issues of substantive representation. In chapter 4 we examine the role of agenda setting. This is an act often related to acts of descriptive, symbolic, and substantive representation. We demonstrate that the members of the LLBC spend more time dealing with issues related to the black community, in particular issues related to racial policy. However, all legislators have very similar agendas on the broad issues they consider. Chapter 5 moves to legislative outcomes and the fate of the proposed bills examined in chapter 4. We show that members of the LLBC are the least likely to have their legislation become law, regardless of the content of the bill. Finally, in chapter 6 we examine voting coalitions in the state legislature. Using a variety of empirical tests, we show that while the LLBC is the most cohesive voting unit in the legislature, it is unable to work across racial and party lines to forge winning coalitions.

In the conclusion we put our findings into the context of the current political reality across the country and discuss potential implications for the future of black politics in Louisiana and in the country as a whole. Finally, we discuss several issues related to the success and failures of the LLBC and possible scenarios for changing these outcomes in the future.

Research Design and Data

Most studies of black representation and legislative life have taken a crosssectional approach by studying multiple legislatures either at one point in time or over numerous years.[2] Our approach is somewhat different. We provide an in-depth analysis of one legislature over two years: Louisiana during the 2005 and 2006 regular and special legislative sessions. This allows us to take a close look at who the black legislators are; what their views are toward legislative life; and the institutional structure within which they operate. This gives us insight into the views of contemporary black legislators and their challenges and successes in influencing public policy and helping their constituents. We combine this perspective with a detailed analysis of the major steps in enacting legislation: agenda setting and bill introductions, committee and floor outcomes, and voting cohesion and patterns. From this analysis, we gain a fuller understanding of minority roles in American politics than many cross-sectional studies are able to gain.

Louisiana is a unique state with a unique political culture. It provides an interesting backdrop for questions of representation and legislative effectiveness.[3] For readers interested specifically in Louisiana, we hope that we provide enough context and details to highlight the state's uniqueness. For readers interested in minority politics and representation more generally, the black political story in Louisiana is similar to that in most other Deep South states and provides a modern political context comparable to that of most black legislators throughout the country.

Beginning in the fall of 2006, we gained access to members of the Louisiana Legislative Black Caucus. We were able to survey 23 of the 32 members of the LLBC and to conduct in-depth interviews with 20 of the members. To make our analysis relevant to the material we obtained from the surveys and interviews, we compiled data for the sessions the legislators had most recently completed, in 2005 and 2006. This was also the period immediately before and following the Hurricane Katrina disaster of August 2005. While we do not focus directly on the legislative response to the disaster, we do address the issue when it is important to the analysis and illustrative of our broader findings. Louisiana legislators conducted their regular annual sessions in 2005 and 2006, with two special sessions in between. We collected data for each of these four sessions in both the house and the senate.

We collected our data from the Louisiana legislative Internet portal, www.legis.state.la.us/. From this database, we gathered information for all bills introduced during these sessions, along with complete bill histories, summaries, committee assignments, amendments, and roll-call votes. Our next step was to code each piece of legislation. First, we placed each bill in one of 22 broad policy areas. Then we divided the bills into categories related to black-interest legislation, a general black-interest category and a race-specific category for bills directly related to issues of race. More information on our coding process and categories may be found in the appendix.

The data we obtained allow us to explore the ability of blacks to achieve representation in today's America. We couch our questions in terms of the ability of black legislators to represent their constituents throughout the legislative process. We examine the answers to our research questions in two primary ways. First, we directly compare LLBC members to other groups in the legislature in terms of agenda setting, bill passage, and roll-call voting. We break the legislature down into three groups: the LLBC, white Democrats, and Republicans.[4] The Democrats held a safe majority in both chambers, but when we look at them in this context, we see an interesting pattern. In the house, the white Democrats held 40 seats; the LLBC, 23 seats; the Republicans, 41 seats. There was only one Independent. In the senate we find a similar pattern, as the white Democrats held 15 seats; the Republicans, 15; and the LLBC, 9.

Beyond the group comparisons, we analyze the similarities and differences among the black legislators to discuss their varying representational methods. We rely primarily on data from our surveys and interviews for our analysis in chapter 3, but we examine differences within the LLBC in the other empirical chapters as well. Overall, we combine our data on bills with data from our surveys and interviews to uncover both how black legislators perceive their roles as legislators and the influences on their legislative work. We try to present detailed and sophisticated statistical analysis in a manner that is accessible for those who may not have graduate training in statistical methods. For those interested in the methodological and statistical details, more technical discussions are contained in the notes. We have tried to provide a straightforward description of how we produced our results and what they mean.

Conclusion

As the following chapters show, the findings demonstrate important similarities and differences between black and white legislators throughout the legislative process and uncover several conditional factors that influence the ability of black legislators to succeed. Our surveys and interviews reveal that members of the LLBC have similar educational and professional backgrounds to those of white Louisiana legislators. We show that the black legislators share similar perceptions of their role as legislators, while there are some important differences in how they identify their ideology and racial identity. In terms of similarities between LLBC members and other legislators, we find an important conditioning influence for those representing New Orleans. From agenda setting to bill-passage rates, representing New Orleans has an interesting influence on the outcomes for all members. Some of the primary differences between LLBC members and white legislators are in voting cohesion and ideology, with black members showing the most cohesive and ideologically similar voting patterns. Throughout the book, we discuss these findings in detail and use examples to reveal interesting nuances in the dynamics of both successful and unsuccessful attempts at representation by minority legislators.

1

Black Electoral Politics

Any discussion of black electoral politics in America must begin by noting the historic victory of Barack Obama in the 2008 presidential election. Without a doubt, the election of the first black president was an achievement that many thought would never occur in their lifetime.[1] While Obama's victory shows how far we have come as a nation, it does not erase the long political struggle that allowed it to occur. While this book is not about Obama's victory or even elections per se, it is important to understand the historical context in which modern black politicians are able to reach their offices. The history of black electoral politics has involved many twists and turns, and with each success, additional obstacles have appeared. Thus, the long struggle for political access and legislative success beneficial to the black community continues into the present. In this chapter, we highlight some of these electoral events in order to better situate the emergence of legislative black caucuses. We consider the following areas: race, law, and exclusion; the increase in black elected officials; the limits of black electoral success; and the dual-representational function of black legislators. Overall, we trace the electoral environment in which black legislators operate so that we can better understand the legislative world in which they serve.

Race, Law, and Exclusion

In order to understand the present state of black electoral politics, it is important to understand the historical complexities of black voting and political involvement over nearly four hundred years of struggle for equal rights and representation. The first Africans arrived in the United States about 1619, not as slaves but as indentured servants[2] who were permitted to vote in 11 of the 13 colonies. However, in the mid-1600s six states legalized slavery, with Massachusetts first legalizing African enslavement in 1641 and other states quickly following suit. This shift in policy, at least in the southern colonies, was primarily due to an increase in agriculture. With an economic justification for slavery, the next step was to institutionalize its legality, as the "American Constitution (itself) represented an affirmation of the slave trade and human enslavement."[3]

Several sections of the U.S. Constitution, Supreme Court decisions, and lower-court rulings supported slavery and denied blacks not only citizenship but also the basic rights protected by the very same document. For example, Article I, Section 9, states: "The Migration or Importation of such Persons as any of the States now existing shall think proper to admit, shall not be prohibited by Congress prior to the year one-thousand-eight-hundred and eight, but a Tax or duty may be imposed on such Importation, not exceeding ten dollars for each person."[4] Legally, from that point on, blacks had no social status, no respect or recognition as legitimate human beings (blacks were often described as beasts, brutes, and savages),[5] and no political rights. Blacks were more beneficial to their masters as slaves than as indentured servants, as Frederick Douglass lamented when he asked, "What to the Slave is the Fourth of July?"[6] He continued: "I am not included within the pale of this glorious anniversary! Your high independence only reveals the immeasurable distance between us. The blessings in which you this day rejoice are not enjoyed in common. The rich inheritance of justice, liberty, prosperity, and independence bequeathed by your father is shared by you, not by me. The sunlight that brought life and healing to you, has brought stripes and death to me. The Fourth of July is yours, not mine."[7]

The decision in *Dred Scott v. Sandford* legally differentiated the races and denied blacks equal rights. Dred Scott, a slave, lived with his master, John Emerson, in Missouri, where slavery was legal, and they often spent time in Wisconsin and Illinois, where slavery was prohibited. Upon Emerson's death, Scott sued for his freedom, claiming that he was a free citizen, having spent extended time in free territories that prohibited slavery. However, the U.S. Supreme Court ruled that Scott was still considered a slave and that slaves had no citizenship rights.

In 1896 the U.S. Supreme Court took up the case *Homer Adolph Plessy v. Ferguson,* which challenged the Jim Crow laws in Louisiana. On June 7,

1892, Plessy was sent to jail for sitting in a railroad car reserved for whites. At that time, Louisiana law required blacks to sit in separate railroad cars. The Louisiana Supreme Court decided that Plessy was guilty of riding in the white car, and Plessy appealed the ruling to the U.S. Supreme Court. Judge Henry Brown, writing for the majority, argued:

> That [the Separate Car Act] does not conflict with the Thirteenth Amendment, which abolished slavery . . . is too clear for argument. . . . A statute which implies merely a legal distinction between the white and colored races—a distinction which is founded in the color of the two races, and which must always exist so long as white men are distinguished from the other race by color—has no tendency to destroy the legal equality of the two races. . . . The object of the Fourteenth Amendment was undoubtedly to enforce the absolute equality of the two races before the law, but in the nature of things it could not have been intended to abolish distinctions based upon color, or to enforce social, as distinguished from political equality, or a commingling of the two races upon terms unsatisfactory to either.[8]

In addition, from 1865 to well into the 1970s, through the use of Black Codes and later the Jim Crow laws, state and local governments in the South enacted policies regulating the lives of former slaves. For example, in Alabama, white nurses were not allowed to be in the same room as blacks. In Arizona, whites could not marry blacks; if they did, the marriage was null and void. In Florida, a white could be sent to jail for 12 months or fined $500 for marrying a black; and in Georgia, whites were not allowed to bury blacks. The primary purpose of these laws was to keep blacks and whites separate, thus perpetuating the negative stereotyping of blacks as being inferior.

Access to the Ballot: The Increase in the Number of Black Elected Officials

During Reconstruction (1867–77), dramatic policy changes occurred involving the newly freed slaves that provided them a glimpse of an American society in which they would have equal access to the political system. Starting with the Thirteenth, Fourteenth, and Fifteenth Amendments and extending to the Civil Rights Act of 1866, the Reconstruction Act of 1867, and the Civil Rights Act of 1875, the newly freed slaves found opportunities and access to the political system available to them as black politicians served in every area of government. Between 1870 and 1875, 14 blacks won election to the U.S. House of Representatives, while Mississippi appointed 2 black U.S. senators, Hiram Rhodes Revels (1870–71) and Blanche Kelso Bruce (1875–81), to serve.[9] All 16 were Republicans. At the state level, six blacks served as lieutenant governors, and there was broad black representation in state legislatures. For example, at one point 76 of the 124 members of the South Carolina House of Representatives were black.[10] However, this success was short lived, as the Compromise of 1877 ended any hopes of equality for blacks in the South.

In agreeing to the Compromise of 1877, the federal government withdrew its troops from the South, effectively ending Reconstruction. Quickly, the South reverted to its old ways, forbidding blacks from participating in government and eliminating the newfound power and rights of the previous decade. During this period, blacks had no representation in government, as white southerners, often through laws and intimidation, prevented blacks from voting and participating in electoral politics. Local laws upholding stipulations such as white primaries, grandfather clauses, literacy tests, understanding clauses, and poll taxes automatically disqualified blacks from voting.[11]

From the end of Reconstruction to the 1930s, blacks in the South were shut out of the political process, as Jim Crow was in full swing. However, in the early twentieth century citizen groups began to form to fight for civil rights. Most successful was the National Association for the Advancement of Colored People (NAACP). Founded in 1910, the NAACP developed a legal strategy that slowly chipped away at Jim Crow. For example, in *Lane v. Wilson* (1939) the grandfather clause was deemed unconstitutional, and in *Smith v. Allwright* (1944) the Supreme Court ruled white primaries unconstitutional. With the eradication of these laws, blacks began to register to vote. While intimidation remained, black organizations continued their efforts to register black voters. Now that blacks had limited access to the ballots, the next steps were to vote and gain representation. However, it quickly became evident that white politicians were doing nothing for their black constituents; thus, while blacks had gained access to the ballot box, their political conditions remained virtually unchanged.

While these early victories allowed for some participation in electoral politics, it clearly was not enough. The next phase was to move from having access to the ballots to having an equal voice in gaining representation. The 1965 Voting Rights Act (VRA) stands out as the most important piece of legislation in this area. By "allowing voters, regardless of race, to register and vote, free from political intimidation and violence," the VRA was the catalyst for a drastic increase in the number of black elected officials throughout the United States.[12] From effectively no black representation in 1960, the number of black elected officials grew to nearly 1,500 in 1970 and has since seen more than a sixfold increase, with more than 9,000 black elected officials at the start of the twenty-first century.[13]

Black Mayors and City Council Members

Blacks have been quite successful at entering political life at the local level. A detailed examination by the Joint Center for Political and Economic Studies found that blacks have had great success in getting elected as city council members and mayors, especially in the southern states. Other than Illinois and Michigan, the states with the most elected black officials are Texas, Mississippi, Louisiana, Georgia, South Carolina, Arkansas, North Carolina, and Alabama.

Since 1974 the number of black elected officials at the local level (mayors, council members, school board members, and superintendents) has more than doubled, from 2,724 to 5,815.[14] For example, in 1974 in the 11 southern states (Alabama, Arkansas, Florida, Georgia, Louisiana, Mississippi, North Carolina, South Carolina, Tennessee, Texas, and Virginia) there were 533 black city council members, compared with 2,466 in 2000.[15] This increase has been due partly to changes in racial composition, electoral structure, and socioeconomic status.[16] For example, where there is a large population of blacks, black candidates who seek city council positions more often than not are elected. While the position of council member is often seen as "less prestigious" and "less powerful," it does provide some "legislative authority," especially over municipal financing. However, the success of black candidates is often thwarted by the fact that they are unsuccessful at winning the seat of city council president, as voting is often very clearly along racial lines. While blacks may win the majority of black precincts, whites usually win the election because of greater voter turnout from their constituency.[17]

A substantial number of black mayors have been elected since the passage of the 1965 Voting Rights Act. For example, in 1974 in the 11 southern states, there were 46 black mayors in office; by 2000 the number had increased to 308.[18] Initially black mayors in the South represented small towns, with only 2 of the 46 in 1974 representing cities with a population greater than 100,000.[19] In 2000, by contrast, 12 black mayors represented cities of more than 100,000 people.[20] Over time, black mayors have found success not only in small southern cities but in large urban areas in the South as well. It is important to note that a major reason for this newfound success in the large cities is due to shifts in demographics. White flight from the cities to the suburbs in the 1970s and 1980s gave blacks an opportunity to get elected. Overall, most local black officials represent majority black constituencies and deal with similar challenges, such as high rates of poverty and unemployment, homelessness, and crime.[21]

Black Governors, State Legislators, and Members of Congress

Surprisingly, the history of the blacks holding the higher offices of governor, legislator, and congressman reaches back further than the history of black mayoral leadership. Between the years 1775 and 1819 there were black governors in Massachusetts, Rhode Island, and Connecticut. While these blacks were elected to governorships (though they only represented certain regions of the state), they did not have the formal power and authority that state governors have today. Their sole purpose was to act as "mediators" between the black and white communities.[22] One should not, however, minimize their role, for they had "substantial responsibilities."[23] Since the passage of the Voting Rights Act of 1965, only two black governors—L. Douglas Wilder, of Virginia, and Deval Patrick, of Massachusetts—have been directly elected; David Paterson, of New York, was originally elected lieutenant governor, becoming governor with the resignation of Eliot Spitzer. L. Douglas Wilder was elected the sixty-fifth governor of Virginia on January 13, 1990; before that, he was the first black elected lieutenant governor of Virginia. In 2006 Deval Patrick became governor of Massachusetts, and he won reelection in 2010. While there has been little success in electing blacks to governorships and limited success in electing blacks to other statewide constitutional offices, the Civil Rights Act of 1965 has had a tremendous impact on the election of black state legislators.

For the year 2000, the Joint Center for Political and Economic Studies reported 142 black state senators and 429 black state representatives.[24] For the most part, the number of black legislators continues to increase at a greater rate in the South than in any other part of the country. For example, in 2007 there were more than 30 black legislators in Georgia (55), Mississippi (46), South Carolina (35), Alabama (34), and Louisiana (32).[25] The vast majority of these legislators were from districts with a black majority and poor districts with low educational achievement and high crime.

In the last forty years, the number of blacks in Congress has also increased dramatically: from 9 in 1970 to 40 in 2010. This has been especially true of black women members, whose numbers rose from just 1 in 1991 to 13 in 2010, with a peak of 15 in 2001.[26] The biggest jump in black members of Congress, from 1991 to 1993, "reflects the impact of the Voting Rights Act of 1965, as the 1990 round of redistricting produced increased numbers of majority-black and majority-minority (black plus Latino) districts."[27]

Only three black candidates have been elected to the U.S. Senate, however: Edward Brooke, of Massachusetts, in 1967; Carol Moseley Braun, of Illinois, in 1992; and Barack Obama, of Illinois, in 2004. This reflects a similar trend in the struggles of blacks to win statewide offices as they lose the benefit of majority-minority districts, which play a major role in the electoral success of state legislators and representatives.

Prior to Barack Obama's historic victory in the 2008 presidential election, several black candidates ran unsuccessful campaigns for the office. In 1972 Shirley Chisholm (the former representative from the Twelfth District in New York) was a candidate for the Democratic nomination.[28] Not only was her race an impediment but her gender was also an important factor in her defeat. Chisholm received roughly 150 of 1,600 delegate votes at the Miami convention; many of the delegates supported either Senator Hubert Humphrey or Senator George McGovern.

Jesse Jackson made a run for the Democratic nomination in 1984 and again in 1988, losing to Walter Mondale in 1984 and to Michael Dukakis in 1988. Alan Keyes, a Republican, routinely runs for president; however, he has never been considered a viable candidate. The one success story has been Barack Obama. It is too early to tell whether his victory marks a change in the ability of black candidates to win state and national elections or is the exception to the rule.

The rise in the number of black elected officials has leveled off in the past decade as the use of majority-minority districts, which led to a major increase from the 1980s to 1990s, has become a staple of the redistricting process. Indeed, the Voting Rights Act of 1965 increased the number of black elected officials, providing blacks unprecedented access to the political system. However, these successes have not come without limitations.

The Limits of Black Electoral Success

The creation of majority-minority districts followed the Supreme Court's decision in *Thornburg v. Gingles* (1986), which established the maximum number of majority-minority districts for geographic areas containing large, politically cohesive minority groups.[29] As Lucius Baker, Mack H. Jones, and Katherine Tate wrote in 1999, "*Gingles* had an enormous effect on legislative districting at all levels, . . . as mapmakers sought to draw plans that complied with the Section 2 of the Voting Rights Act as interpreted by the Supreme Court in *Gingles*. While the Court's subsequent restrictions on race-based districting have created some ambiguity regarding the contours of Section 2 and the viability of *Gingles* precedent, it remains clear that for now, the shadow of *Gingles* will continue to loom over redistricting efforts."[30]

During the 105th Session of the U.S. Congress, 24 of the 37 black members were from majority-black congressional districts, while several additional black representatives were from majority-minority districts. Very few of the black elected officials came from majority-white districts. In essence, "the constituencies represented by black members of Congress tend to be mostly black."[31]

In 2000 a record number of black candidates (29) ran in majority-white districts for state-level offices, but only 9 were successful. Of 11 black candidates for statewide elective office in 2000, only 4 won.[32] At the congressional level, only 1 percent of the blacks are from majority-white districts.[33] While black candidates do run outside of majority-black and majority-minority districts, they fail much more often than they succeed.

With the widespread use of majority-minority districts, blacks have come close to achieving descriptive representation, or having the same percentage of seats in a legislative body as their percentage of the general population, in the House of Representatives but fall short in most states. For example, Georgia has the largest number of black legislators (55), but they account for only 23 percent of the entire legislative body, while blacks make up 30 percent of the state population. Similarly in Louisiana, the state was roughly 32 percent black, but the 32 black legislators made up only 22.2 percent of the state legislature during the period under study. Overall, despite the gains in winning elections over the past two decades, black legislators still do not provide effective representation, at least from the standpoint of proportionally representing their constituents in the legislature.

Despite the low likelihood of being elected outside of majority-black and majority-minority districts, many blacks still pursue these offices. Two such cases are especially interesting and have received a great deal of attention from scholars. The 1990 U.S. Senate election in North Carolina pitted an incumbent white candidate, Republican Jesse Helms, against a black newcomer, Democrat Harvey Gantt. Several things went right for Gantt: (1) he secured a unified party backing; (2) he created a multiracial coalition; (3) he pursued a "de-racialized" campaign, emphasized a "personal style," and "avoided divisive issues"; (4) he had a campaign war chest nearly equal to Helms's; and (5) he did not get involved in a negative campaign. So how is it that he lost the race? First, Helms ran a negative campaign. Second, Gantt was not able to get a substantial amount of the white support. Third, and most important, Gantt's race and race-related issues played a central role in his defeat.[34]

Andrew Young was defeated in the same year. Upon completion of his term as mayor of Atlanta, Young decided to run for the governorship of Georgia. He had name recognition, but black voter turnout remained low in Georgia, and previous corruption among black elected officials had hurt the group's reputation.[35] In addition to these obstacles, which were not of his doing, Young had other shortcomings. For example, he was viewed as an "outsider"; there were "ideological problems"; and he "adopted a passive position on capital punishment, crime and law enforcement, drug policy, and the saliency of race."[36]

Two other black candidates had wide support from the political establishment but nevertheless lost statewide races in 2000. Ron Kirk lost to John Cornyn in the Texas Senate race, and H. Carl McCall lost the governorship of New York to the incumbent, George Pataki. In all of these states, it has been very difficult for black candidates to win elections to offices in which they would represent white majorities. Where does the blame lie? Many scholars suggest that racial stereotyping of black candidates presents some of the most persuasive evidence for the limits of black electoral success; however, not everyone is convinced by the findings that racial stereotyping plays a role in elections.

Racial Stereotyping and Electoral Implications

Understanding the origins of stereotypes is an important part of understanding black electoral politics, because several major scholarly investigations have identified racial stereotyping as an impediment to black electoral success. The concept of social categorization is central to the discussion of stereotyping. Susan Fiske argues that "humans inevitably categorize objects and people in their world, and that to prejudge is entirely normal." For example, "just as people categorize furniture into tables and chairs, putting their drinks on one and sitting on the other, so too, people categorize each other into in-groups and out-groups, loving one and hating the other."[37] As Gordon Allport describes it, "Impressions that are similar, especially if a label is attached, tend to cohere into categories. All categories engender meaning upon the world. Like paths in a forest, they give order to our lifespace. The principle of least effort inclines us to hold to coarse and early-formed generalizations as long as they can possibly be made to serve our purposes. An ethnic prejudice is a category concerning a group of people, not based on defining attributes primarily, but including various 'noisy' attributes, leading to a disparagement of the group as a whole."[38]

Several theories explain stereotyping as a predictable by-product of the normal cognitive process, especially categorization. The argument has been made that "people are cognitive misers, overwhelmed by the complexity of the social environment and forced to conserve scarce mental resources."[39] According to Shelley Taylor, categorization, a cognitive shortcut, is useful in that it "1) tags information by physical and social distinctions such as race and gender; 2) minimizes within-group differences and exaggerates between-group differences; and 3) causes group members' behavior to be interpreted stereotypically."[40] The process of categorizing people into groups brings out "more distinctions among the groups and gives rise to more stereotyped perceptions."[41] Nevertheless, while categorization is a useful cognitive shortcut, "automatic categorization and automatic associations to categories are the major culprits in the endurance of stereotyping."[42]

Social stereotypes have been defined as the "cognitive structures that contain the perceiver's knowledge, beliefs, and expectations about human groups";[43] these cognitive structures affect the encoding and processing of information pertaining to out-group members. In particular, stereotypes are a type of schema, or "pictures in the head," simplified mental images of what groups look like and what they do. Stereotypes can be either negative or positive, but even positive stereotypes can have negative consequences. Nevertheless, stereotypes are always inaccurate, because they are never true of all group members at all times.

The formation of stereotypes can occur through personal interaction (i.e., attention to extremes, illusory correlation, and social roles) and social learning (i.e., from others and from the media). According to scholars working in the area of social cognition, the information we gain either from personal interaction or from social learning results in the "production of stereotypes that help us simplify our environment, thus teaching and reinforcing certain ideas about groups."[44] Depending on how they are depicted, these stereotypes can have a negative impact on how certain groups are perceived.

Thus, the formation of black stereotypes is a product of social learning, either from others or from the media. The seeds of negative stereotypes of blacks were planted in part as a result of the decisions made by the U.S. government, in particular creating and highlighting negative distinctions based on race as soon as blacks arrived in the country as slaves. In addition to the negative stereotypes of blacks embedded in law, the media has perpetuated stereotypes of blacks, and media stereotyping can influence electoral politics. According to a 2000 study, half of all teens spend at least six hours a week watching television, and adults watch an average of 2.1 hours of television per day.[45] Thus, how blacks are depicted on television may affect viewers' perceptions. In general, blacks have been portrayed in the media as "1) the mammy—a good, wholesome caretaker of whites, yet a mean and insensitive presence in her own family; 2) the coon—representing black ineptness at living successfully in white society; 3) the Tom—an apologist for slavery; and finally 4) the Buck—the violent and uncontrollable black."[46]

Especially on television, blacks are depicted as "criminals, drug dealers, and gang members."[47] Network news portrays "ghettoized" blacks. Increasingly, blacks appear mostly in crime, sports, and entertainment stories; rarely are blacks shown making important contributions to the serious business of the nation. For example, Robert M. Entman and Andrew Rojecki found during the 1990s that a substantial portion of the news coverage was devoted to violent crimes committed by blacks. More important, media presentations of black and white criminals differed: "the former were more likely to be named, be seen in handcuffs in physical custody, and were less likely to speak for themselves."[48] In addition, blacks were more likely to be portrayed as criminals and as physically threatening;[49] specifically, black female characters were shown using "vulgarity 89% of the time; being physically violent 56% of the time; and being restrained 55% of the time."[50]

In television ads, "hidden patterns of differentiation and distance emerge; for instance, blacks do not touch whites in ads, but (unlike whites) they rarely even touch each other, conveying a subtle message of black skin as taboo."[51] For example, in magazine advertisements, "advertisers are considerably less likely to use blacks as their examples of high status consumers than whites";[52] furthermore, blacks are also shown in subordinate relationship roles to whites.

Blacks are overrepresented in the media as athletes and musicians.[53] For example, if blacks appear on television news programs, they are more likely to be sports reporters. In a study of local television news programs from 22 cities, blacks tended not to appear as on-camera news sources or reporters or be included in news stories about nonracial issues.[54]

In the end, scholars argue that these depictions, which perpetuate stereotypes of blacks, can have the effect of "communicating misinformation about blacks; this misinformation is then used by whites to make social judgments about blacks," particularly when evaluating black candidates. For example, survey research has consistently shown that in comparison with other racial groups, blacks have been stereotyped as lazy, poor, violent, unintelligent, and welfare-dependent. Mark Peffley and Jon Hurwitz's 1997 study revealed that 31 percent of the respondents accepted blacks as lazy, 40 percent characterized blacks as complainers, and 50 percent called blacks aggressive. In addition, "whites' attitudes toward crime are likely to be tied to their global stereotypes of blacks, with whites who see blacks as characteristically violent displaying a more punitive view on issues such as rehabilitation, prison, furloughs, and sentencing, at least when such policies are targeted for blacks."[55]

The "images whites have of blacks are consequential because they affect other attitudes toward these groups. For example, whites who view blacks as lazy and welfare-dependent are significantly less likely than other whites to support government programs designed to help blacks escape from poverty."[56] In other words, "so long as whites believe that blacks lack a work ethic, are prone to criminal activity, and are less intelligent than whites, they will disparage them as neighbors."[57]

To return to our original argument, it is important to realize that these attitudes can become a heuristic used by voters to judge candidates. For example, race was a relevant factor in voting decisions during the 1982 California gubernatorial race between Tom Bradley (the black candidate) and George Deukmejian (the white candidate).[58] Specifically, the black candidate was stereotyped as the liberal who favored big government and was soft on crime.[59]

In fact, skin color has been shown to affect voter preferences. In experimental settings, the darker the candidate's skin tone, the less likely he or she is to win.[60] Additionally, the "anti-black effect had significant effects on Jesse Jackson" during his presidential campaigns,[61] and some studies have shown that black candidates were seen as less capable of handling major policy issues.[62]

In the end, voters use stereotypes to fill in the blanks when they know only a little about a candidate. In the words of Murray Edelman, "We are often unable to see the whole picture and so make decisions that are based on a small part of the relevant total." Particularly in situations where voters are told that a candidate is black, whites are likely to use racial stereotypes to guide them in their decision making. "Images shape thoughts about politics, and influence action; for highly important decisions, then, images are crucial."[63] The stereotypes, for example, that blacks are less competent than whites, that minority members are lacking in policy-management skills, and that black candidates are liberals who favor big government and are soft on crime could collectively have a big impact on an individual's voting behavior.[64] The media's negative depictions of blacks can be used as stereotypes by whites in making judgments, especially about blacks running for office.

Overall, empirical research suggests that we use stereotypes, group categorization, and other simplifying techniques to simplify our complex social environment; however, a major result of this cognitive process is intergroup bias or discrimination, which greatly thwarts an increase in black electoral representation. On the other hand, some scholars contend that racial stereotyping is not a sufficient explanation for the failure of black candidates to win outside of majority-black cities and majority-minority districts; the real culprit for black electoral failure, they argue, is the political campaign strategy employed by black candidates.

Political Campaign Strategy: Causes of Black Electoral Failure

Many scholars contend that a candidate's campaign strategy is probably the most important factor contributing to political success; indeed, the tone of a campaign and the way a candidate is perceived by the public can be key to a candidate's success. Speaking to the relevancy of race in elections, Carol Swain points out that "black candidates fail to take account of a key electoral fact: candidates run as individuals and not as categorical groups; [thus,] it is possible for someone to dislike a group, but to make exceptions for individual group members."[65] In other words, blacks are not successful because of the type of political campaigns they run.

In her detailed study of black representation, *Black Faces, Black Interests* (1993), Swain explains that black representatives who follow a prescribed campaign method can find success regardless of their race. She describes in detail the electoral strategies of three black representatives who won election in majority-white districts: Alan Wheat (D-MO), Katie Hall (D-IN), and Ron Dellums (D-CA). All three formed biracial and multicultural coalitions; were aware of and responsive to varied interests, not just black interests; possessed the sophistication to speak to all voters; forged personal interaction with all voters; gained endorsements from prominent members of the community; based their campaigns on issues rather than on race; were from a high social class and had a high education level; had a positive image; and, finally, refrained from engaging in racially inflammatory speeches or calling for black solidarity.

Another case study of successful black candidates compared the statewide elections of Edward Brooke, L. Douglas Wilder, and Tom Bradley.[66] From these races we learn that black candidates must exhibit a moderate racial attitude. This is most important for winning the nomination and makes election plausible. The campaign strategy must be able to captivate both black and white voters. Further, the political style must be "quiet and conciliating."[67]

In the end, those who argue that campaign strategy is more important than racial stereotypes as a factor in elections point to the elections of Barack Obama and other successful candidates as evidence. Specifically, Obama and the other successful candidates mentioned above fulfilled some of the conditions for a winning political campaign by gaining endorsements from prominent black and white members of the community and from a wide variety of political, business, and service organizations; forming a campaign team that included a wide spectrum of people; gaining the backing of the political establishment; and running a deracialized political campaign (i.e., a campaign based on issues rather than on race); and possessing previous political experience.

The notion that black candidates who follow a deracialized campaign strategy tend to have more success is especially interesting. In the 1989 mayoral and gubernatorial elections, "four of the nine successful candidates ran deracialized campaigns."[68] What exactly does it mean to "deracialize"? Roger Oden defines *deracialization* by "black electoral candidates in majority white districts and jurisdictions" as "deemphasiz[ing] racial themes in their campaigns in order to maximize their chances of attracting enough white votes to win elections."[69] It is important to mention here that simply courting white voters through the use of race-neutral policies does not mean that the black candidates' ideas about race-related issues have changed. They just choose not to emphasize those ideas, since doing so could potentially alienate white voters. To highlight this point, Judson Jeffries, in his evaluation of the elections of Edward Brooke and L. Douglas Wilder, found that they did not "wear their blackness on their sleeve; instead, they presented themselves as candidates who happened to be black." As Edward Brooke explained, "I wanted to be perceived as a qualified candidate, not a black candidate." Instead of focusing on their race, both Brooke and Wilder "emphasized those issues that transcended race and appealed to a broad spectrum of the electorate, like the economy, education, transportation, abortion, education, health care, and the environment."[70]

How do a black candidate's race-neutral positions on issues affect the black electorate's views of the candidate? In their campaigns, both Brooke and Wilder distanced themselves from the "civil rights movement and civil rights activists." Wilder even stated, "I have never been a civil rights activist of any kind. I have tried to work within the courts." When it came to the discussion of issues such as affirmative action and welfare, Brooke argued that "government handouts were not the way to remedy the plight of the disadvantaged," and when affirmative action was mentioned, Wilder explained that "encouraging economic growth was the best method for lifting those who had yet to experience the prosperity of the 1980s."[71]

This strategy resulted in victory for both men, as they carried both the white and the black vote. "Not only did Wilder garner 41 percent of the white vote," writes Alvin Schexnider, "but two-thirds of his total votes came from whites, and even more astonishing is the fact that he received 25 percent of the conservative votes and one-third of the voters who helped to elect George Bush in 1988."[72] And even though Wilder evaded discussing race-centered policies, he captured 96 percent of the black vote.[73] In the end, by taking race-neutral positions, black candidates can gain the support of both the black and the white electorate, which often leads to electoral victory. However, the policy decisions they make once in office depend on the way they see the world. Many suggest that deracialized campaigns are evidence that "black politics is not maturing, but it may be degenerating."[74]

What creates black electoral successes and failures is the subject of an ongoing debate. On the one side are those who argue that racial stereotyping is a major factor; on the other side are those who argue that success or failure is attributable not to race but to the candidate's campaign strategy. What is known is that the success rate of black candidates running in majority-white areas is very low, and this has important implications for the policymaking process: the election of black candidates is essential because of their dual-representational function.

The Dual-Representational Function of Black Elected Officials

One of the most important outcomes of electing minorities to office is that they bring diversity to those holding positions of power and make it possible for minority constituents to identify racially with their elected leaders, as race can be a "signal that speaks louder than words, or at least with more meaning."[75] The notion that leaders share certain characteristics of those whom they represent is termed *descriptive representation*. It refers to "how a legislator looks."[76] According to Jane Mansbridge, it "aids in achieving deliberative synergy, critical mass, dispersion of influence, and a range of views within the group."[77]

Descriptive representation provides for a variety of perspectives, opinions, and interests in the deliberative process. Blacks with different ideological and political persuasions provide important benefits during deliberations. As Mansbridge writes,

> [Blacks] in the United States are far more richly represented deliberatively by a Congress that includes William Gray III (a black member of Congress who did not support the Congressional Black Caucus's alternative budget because he was chairman of the Budget Committee in the House) and George Crockett (a Black member of Congress who condemned the State Department for refusing to grant Yasir Arafat an entry visa) than by a Congress that included only one of these two—because it provides for diversity in opinions and styles within the spectrum of black representation in Congress.[78]

Marie Redd, a black West Virginia state senator, explained, "There's no one there [in the West Virginia state legislature] who knows what it's like to be a minority in West Virginia. There's no one there for the insight of the minority view."[79]

Descriptive representation aids in the articulation of diverse points of view in the legislative process and influences the member-constituent relationship.[80] Descriptive representation can "forge bonds of trust between legislator and constituent, enhancing the feeling of inclusion, which, in turn, makes the polity democratically more legitimate in one's eyes."[81] For example, black control of the mayor's office can enhance political trust among black citizens, contributing to a more favorable impression of city government as a whole.[82] Descriptive representation can facilitate the "vertical communication" between representatives and constituents. For instance, black constituents are more likely to contact their representative if that representative is black.[83] New Jersey Representative Donald Payne's view that "black constituents feel comfortable with me, and see that I feel comfortable with them" captures this relationship.[84]

Another benefit of descriptive representation is the construction of social meaning and "de facto legitimacy." Regarding the construction of social meaning, Mack H. Jones found that the political culture of the South was shifting toward the "idea of blacks as political participants rather than subjects" due to the growing number of blacks being elected to office.[85] In addition, "blacks will see other blacks succeeding in society; they will be role models to the black youth of the nation."[86]

In reference to de facto legitimacy, Mansbridge writes that

> seeing proportional numbers of members of their group can enhance de facto legitimacy by making citizens, and particularly members of historically underrepresented groups feel as if they themselves were present in the deliberations.... To a great degree this benefit is a consequence of previous ones. Easier communication with one's representative, awareness that one's interests are being represented with sensitivity, and knowledge that certain features of one's identity do not mark one as less able to govern all contribute to making one feel more included in the polity. This feeling of inclusion in turn makes the polity democratically more legitimate in one's eye. Having had a voice in making of a particular policy, even if that voice is through one's representative and even when one's views do not prevail, also makes policy more legitimate in one's eyes.[87]

While descriptive representation can build public trust and construct social meaning and de facto legitimacy, it can also promote political participation. Katherine Tate found that blacks who were represented by blacks were likely to know more about their legislators than those represented by whites. Nearly one-quarter of the respondents represented by a black member of Congress could identify him or her by name, compared with "only 8 to 10 percent of those represented by whites." Additionally, blacks represented by blacks "expressed greater interest in politics than those represented by whites."[88] Furthermore, Tate found that "blacks consistently express higher levels of satisfaction with their representation in Washington when that representative is black, even controlling for other characteristics of the legislators."[89] Descriptive representation has positive results: it creates opportunity for diverse opinions in deliberations; positively affects member-constituent relationships (e.g., forging bonds of trust and producing feelings of inclusion); produces more constituent satisfaction with representatives; and results in more knowledge and interest in politics on the part of constituents.

In addition to *descriptive* representation, black elected officials provide *substantive* representation to their constituents. Substantive representation "is enacting legislation that furthers the interests of the minority community,"[90] or simply how the legislator "acts."[91] The most common form of substantive representation is roll-call voting but it also includes casework in the district and taking part in the deliberative process. Some scholars contend that descriptive representation produces substantive representation. Mansbridge argues that "when interests are un-crystallized (such as those issues involving gender and race), the best way to have one's most important substantive interests represented is often to choose a representative whose descriptive characteristics match one's own on the issues one expects to emerge." Through this horizontal communication, she suggests, "a descriptive representative can draw on elements of experiences shared with constituents to explore the uncharted ramifications of newly presented issues and also speak on those issues with a voice carrying the authority of experience."[92]

Note that Mansbridge defines substantive representation in terms of being able to convey information during deliberations by those who share similar experiences. For example, in Richard Fenno's seminal work, *Home*

Style, he quotes a black legislator as saying that "when I vote my conscience as a black man, I necessarily represent the black community. I don't have any trouble knowing what the black community thinks or wants."[93]

More recent research also contends that descriptive representation produces substantive results. Kathleen Bratton and Kerry Haynie write that "race exerts a powerful influence on the introduction of black interest bills; black legislators introduce more black interest bills than do other legislators."[94] They found that black lawmakers have a distinct policymaking focus, and "bill sponsorship is influenced not only by a legislator's party and constituency, but also by the legislator's race."[95]

In other examples of substantive policy gains through demographic representation, Kathryn Yatrakis found that the black mayor of Newark, New Jersey, provided significant policy benefits to the black community.[96] Rufus Browning, Dale Rogers Marshall, and David Tabb concluded that the presence of minorities on local councils reduced polarization and stereotyping and also led to "the creation of police review boards, the appointments of more minorities to commissions, the increased use of minority contractors, and a general increase in the number of programs oriented toward minorities."[97]

On the other hand, some scholars disagree that black elected officials provide positive benefits for their constituents in the form of descriptive and substantive representation. Carol Swain argues that an increase in the number of black elected officials has not improved the quality of the representative relationship for black constituents. The interaction of black elected officials with their constituents, according to Swain, has become "complacent, they often view themselves as trustees, possess an individualistic style (which allows them to advance their own political agendas), and they usually do not consult with their constituents."[98] Much of this is because "the descriptive characteristics of the representative can lull voters into thinking their substantive interests are being represented even when this is not the case."[99] One black representative told Swain that "one of the advantages, and disadvantages, of representing blacks is their shameless loyalty to their incumbents. You can almost get away with raping babies and be forgiven. You don't have any vigilance about your performance."[100]

Furthermore, empirical studies have revealed that descriptive representation does not necessarily yield substantive representation. David Epstein and Sharyn O'Halloran explain that while racial redistricting in South Carolina has increased the number of black representatives at the local and national levels, it has adversely affected the overall support for minority-favored legislation; that is, it has contributed to the lack of support from nonblack members of Congress.[101] Epstein, O'Halloran, and Charles Cameron claim that a trade-off exists between substantive and descriptive representation:

> Some would argue that there is an independent value to having minority representatives in office, making Congress look more like the population it represents. On the other hand, past a certain point, an increase in the number of minority representatives comes at the cost of votes in favor of minority-sponsored legislation. It is disconcerting that no minorities were elected to Congress from the South between 1898 and 1972. But it is hard to argue that minority voters in Georgia are better served today overall when their congressional delegation goes from nine Democrats and one Republican to three black Democrats and eight white Republicans in the span of two years. Thus, there is a trade-off to be made, striking a balance between electing minority representatives to office and enacting legislation favored by the minority community.[102]

However, Christian Grose argues that many scholars define substantive representation in the very narrow terms of roll-call voting and do not address the multiple activities that members of Congress engage in. He found that descriptive representation yields substantive representation (including pork to districts and constituency services) when measured as activities beyond roll-call voting.[103]

In sum, it can be argued that black elected officials provide not only descriptive but also substantive representation. They can offer a variety of perspectives, opinions, and interests in the deliberative process; construct social meaning and de facto legitimacy; give constituency services and pork to districts; and initiate policy that focuses on the needs of their black and other minority constituents. Overall, most scholars suggest a trade-off between the benefits and costs of increased descriptive representation and the ability to provide substantive representation.

Conclusion

Modern black politics continues to evolve, from the passage of the Voting Rights Act to the rise of majority-minority districting practices to the election of Barack Obama as president. With each step forward come additional challenges. In many respects, overcoming these current challenges (i.e., increasing the number of black elected officials and securing positive public policy) is going to be important for bettering the lives of blacks, especially through their participation in the legislative process. As we continue our evaluation of the successes and failures of black elected officials in the Louisiana legislature, we must keep in mind the history and context within which they operate in order to understand and appreciate their achievements and disappointments. We now turn to the institutional response of black legislative officials in attempts to secure the positive public policy their officeholding affords.

2
An Overview of Black Caucus History

Once blacks began to have electoral success, the next step was to translate it into policy success. This has proved to be difficult. Even though blacks began to gain electoral victories, they remained the minority in all but some local institutions and had to find ways to work within the institutions while focusing on their core mission of representing the underrepresented. The Congressional Black Caucus (CBC) and counterparts at the state level best exemplify the legislative and policy goals of black elected officials. In 2001, Eddie Bernice Johnson (D-TX), then chair of the CBC, captured the need and purpose of these groups when she stated in the House, "Mr. Speaker, our being here is not an individual accomplishment, it is a testament to a people. Blacks in this country have gone from chains to Congress. . . . As members of the Congressional Black Caucus, our motto has always been 'No permanent friends, no permanent enemies, just permanent issues.'"[1]

From the onset of slavery, various groups have emerged to challenge the inequalities faced by blacks. In this chapter we discuss some of the groups that were instrumental in challenging these inequalities. We focus on black political conventions, political parties, and protest organizations. Again, we highlight only a handful of these organizations to situate the black caucuses in the historical context that brought them about. We then explore the emergence of the national and state legislative black caucuses, focusing on the formation and purpose of the CBC and state legislative black caucuses, as well as the historical development and institutionalization of the Louisiana Legislative Black Caucus (LLBC).

The Emergence of Black Political Conventions, Political Parties, and Protest Organizations

Formal black conventions began to emerge in the 1830s; however, smaller, informal gatherings began well before that and lasted well into the 1970s. There were major national and state conventions whose purpose was to discuss, debate, and devise strategies for ameliorating the conditions of blacks. These conventions have been pivotal in the development of black politics, for regardless of the era in which these meetings were held, they "gave black men and women a sense of identity, and a feeling of confidence and self-respect."[2] Nor should the courage of those in attendance be overlooked, as especially in the early years "many delegates risked their lives to attend, for gangsters dogged their footsteps, and mobs were organized to break up the conventions."[3] Nevertheless, for many of the delegates the cause was worth the risk.

The first such convention began on September 20, 1830, in Philadelphia. The convention lasted 10 days; the delegates met in secret the first 5 days, while the remainder of the convention was made public. Forty black delegates from nine states attended. Richard Allen was selected the president of the conference, which was called the National Negro Convention. Allen, a former slave, had purchased his freedom and become an influential member of the Methodist denomination. In his "Address to the Free People of Colour of these United States," Allen stated that "our forlorn and deplorable situation earnestly and loudly demand of us to devise and pursue all legal means for the speedy elevation of ourselves and brethren to the scale and standing of men."[4] Allen suggested that in order to accomplish these goals, blacks should form societies under the general convention. There was some disagreement among those in attendance regarding how these societies would function. Many of the discussions at this and similar conventions in the 1830s were about assimilation, whose supporters argued that working *within the system* was the most effective way to show whites that blacks deserved equal standing in American society. In his address, Allen set out specific recommendations:

> It is to obviate these evils, that we have recommended our views to our fellow-citizens in the foregoing instrument, with a desire of

raising the moral and political standing of ourselves; and we cannot devise any plan more likely to accomplish this end, than by encouraging agriculture and mechanical arts: for by the first, we shall be enabled to act with a degree of independence, which as yet has fallen to the lot of but few among us; and the faithful pursuit of the latter, in connection with the sciences, which expand and ennoble the mind, will eventually give us the standing and condition we desire.[5]

Heeding Allen's call, most of the subsequent conventions of the 1840s focused on working within the system, thus extending the discussions of the 1830s conventions; however, some conventions challenged the goal of assimilation and argued for slave insurrections as the best means of attaining freedom. The agenda for those conventions that favored assimilation was "temperance, education, economy, agricultural and mechanical trades, and development of a manual labor school."[6] The two major conventions held in the 1840s dealt with the establishment of a black press and how best to abolish slavery. On August 15, 1843, in Buffalo, New York, 30 delegates, mostly from the Northeast, met to discuss these two topics. On the establishment of a black press, there was no consensus by the end of the convention. On the abolition of slavery, discussion focused on the use of physical violence to reach this goal. Two factions emerged, led by Frederick Douglass, who believed in working within the system to abolish slavery, and Henry Highland Garnet, who believed that the only way to end slavery was through insurrection.

The second major convention in the 1940s was held in Troy, New York, on October 6, 1847. The 66 delegates discussed and voted affirmatively on creating a national black press, with the *North Star,* owned by Douglass, serving as their first national black newspaper. In addition, there was initial discussion and support for a separate "manual labor" college for blacks. The conventions of the mid-forties represent "a definite gain for independent [black] leadership." Indeed, "by 1847, even scoffers were forced to admit that the National Negro Convention was once more the most powerful voice in [black] affairs—a voice that had a militant ring which was absent from the deliberations of the thirties, a voice commanding the confidence of the [black] masses and the respect of all men of good will."[7]

In contrast to the general assimilationist philosophies that dominated the 1840s, the 1850s brought a new fervor for black nationalism and emigration among the delegates at the conventions. Two major conventions of the 1850s dealt with these issues. The convention in Rochester, New York, on July 6–8, 1853, brought together some 140 delegates, more than at any of the previous conventions. Douglass presided over the convention, and the major issue of contention, as in previous conventions, was how blacks could best obtain equality in American society. Again there were two schools of thought, one arguing that emigration (or at least separation from the American government and society) was the only way blacks could achieve equality, the other continuing to support assimilationism, arguing that remaining in America and working within the system would eventually prove successful.

While these conventions often generated more conflict than agreement and did not lead to any direct results on the biggest issue of the day, slavery, they did establish a black political voice to debate the issues of the day. As Jane and William Pease have explained, "On the floors of the conventions [during the 1800s], behind the scenes, in the press, and in private letters, black leaders of the antebellum period left a record of competition, rivalry, dispute, and distrust. There is no question that the convention movement provided a forum in which men tested themselves as well as their ideas. In the process, old ideas were refined, new ideas projected, and fresh hopes kindled. Yet, at the same time, both race and movement were weakened by the divisiveness of ideological controversy and the shattering consequences of personal rivalry."[8]

The use of conventions to fight various inequalities in America did not end in the 1800s. Even well into the twentieth century, in 1972, prominent black leaders called for a national black convention in order to "discuss the development of a strategy to maximize the impact of the black vote" in the 1972 presidential election.[9] Some of the prominent leaders who attended the meeting in Gary, Indiana, were Jesse Jackson, John Conyers, Julian Bond, and Willie Brown. The discussions centered on candidate strategy, which called for a black candidate to run in the presidential election in order to nationalize the black vote. In addition, the discussions concentrated on a black agenda, which included the creation of a black party, running a black candidate for president, issues of busing, possible solutions to the Middle East conflict, and voter mobilization. The meeting ended with very little consensus on either of the major issues. Subsequent conventions were held in Gary, Little Rock, Dayton, and Cincinnati, with, again, little agreement. Robert C. Smith explained the shortcoming of a universal convention as follows:

> History confirms in the convention process of the 1830s, 1930s, and 1970s one simple proposition: the black community is too ideologically diverse to operate for long in a single, all-inclusive organization capable of representing the interests of the race in its relationships to whites or the larger external political order. The fundamental error of the conveners of the black conventions of the 1830s, 1930s, and 1970s is the assumption that the common condition of race oppression is sufficient to constitute an objective basis for a political unity that would transcend ideological differences. This is not possible, because ideology is important; dealing as it does with fundamental ideas on the nature, causes, strategies and solutions of the black predicament.[10]

In efforts to make gains within a political system dominated by two parties, blacks forged racially exclusive national parties, state parties, and "protest" organizations. The two major national black political parties that tried to defy the odds and break from the two-party system were the Freedom Now Party, founded in 1963, and the Peace and Freedom Party, founded in 1968. The main goals of the Freedom Now Party were "to elect more militant blacks, make a show of black political power, and educate blacks to use their political power effectively."[11] In 1963 the party entered black candidates in the New York, California, and Connecticut elections; all of the party's candidates were defeated, and the party left little lasting impression on either the black electorate or the general public. Similarly, the Peace and Freedom Party's primary goals included "radical economic programs, black freedom, and peace in Vietnam."[12] Like the Freedom Now Party, the Peace and Freedom Party tried to establish itself as a national political party, but it too failed. At the time, blacks were aware that forming exclusively black political parties was not a realistic goal, because even the black electorate did not support their candidates. Indeed, while these parties failed to gain a lasting place in American politics, they made the black community aware of the importance of participating in politics.

While some blacks fought for black national political parties, other blacks, feeling disenfranchised by the Democratic Party, attempted to create independent black state parties. The Mississippi Freedom Democratic Party and the United Citizens Party (UCP) of South Carolina emerged (with limited success) in response to the Democratic Party's refusal to support black candidates.[13] The objective of the UCP was to elect black candidates on its ticket rather than the Democratic Party ticket; for the most part, however, this effort failed. In the 1970 governor's race in South Carolina, write-in UCP black candidates were added to the Democratic and Republican slates. In the election, the UCP candidates lost by a huge margin, only garnering 0.07 percent of the total votes. However, the party's efforts were not in vain; "its ability to siphon black votes in the majority black counties and precincts that traditionally supported the Democratic Party led the Democratic Party to accommodate the concerns of the UCP members."[14]

Other black leaders looked outside mainstream political party membership to galvanize and unify other blacks to participate in black political life. With the failure of black political parties, black "protest" organizations, such as the NAACP, the Urban League, and the Southern Christian Leadership Conference (SCLC), evolved with the mission to indirectly secure favorable public policy. "Protest" organizations are similar to other political interest groups, as their main function is to persuade legislators to view issues of concern from the perspective of the organization. Traditionally, since black membership in Congress and state legislatures was minimal, "protest" organizations usually had to depend on white legislators. Often the interests of the protest organizations were not aligned with those of white legislators; as a result, gaining favorable public policy was very difficult.

Overall, black conventions, black political parties, and black protest organizations fought for black equality and educated blacks about the importance of participating in politics. Their direct imprint is evident in the positive development of black electoral politics. However, as the number of black elected officials increased in state legislatures across the country, a new political strategy emerged to secure more favorable policy outputs for the black community directly through the legislative process. This new political strategy was the formation of legislative black caucuses at the national and state levels.

What Are Caucuses?

A legislative caucus is a group made up of members of the legislature (at the congressional or state level) whose intent is to represent a specific interest or influence a particular area of policy. Caucuses are divided into party caucuses and nonparty caucuses. Party caucuses include the Republican Conference and the Democratic Caucus (or the majority and minority caucuses, depending on which party holds the majority status at a particular time) in Congress. Party caucuses toil with their party leaders at all stages of the legislative process; they participate in leadership activity, shaping policies that are in line with the goals of the caucus. More important, party caucuses "seek to influence policy without fragmenting the parties." They also help with "coordination and centralization within the legislatures" and provide information for their members.[15]

Nonparty caucuses are "identifiable, self-conscious, relatively stable unit[s] of interacting members whose relationships are not officially prescribed by statutes and rules."[16] These nonparty organizations usually form around a special interest. Nonparty caucuses in Congress number in the hundreds, and the interests they represent range from economic (the Congressional Steel Caucus), regional (the New England Congressional Caucus), and national (the Congressional Black Caucus) to ideological (the recently founded Tea Party Caucus) concerns. According to Burdett A. Loomis, the proliferation of these nonparty groups is "both a response to leadership failure and a challenge to current leadership styles."[17]

In Congress, as these nonparty caucuses focus on achieving their goals, they sometimes work with party leaders while at other times they work against them. These caucuses serve primarily as a psychological support system.[18] They also create an arena in which information can flow easily among members and produce "trustworthy information on bills and legislative politics; cues for making voting decisions; and finally, adaptive norms, perceptions and rationalizations."[19]

The Congressional Black Caucus

The Congressional Black Caucus was founded in 1971; however, its roots extend back to the 1960s, when Charles Diggs formed the Democratic

Select Committee. Considered an informal organization, the CBC, which is an exclusively black organization, was formed to "promote and attempt to preserve legislation salient to black constituents."[20] The essential responsibilities of the CBC are to investigate the issues affecting the black community, lobby for the interests of black constituents, and orient new members to the U.S. Congress.[21]

The CBC began at the "collective stage," implicitly based on the assumption that "black congressmen had special responsibilities and had to play a role that responded to the unique problems of black Americans." Nevertheless, the CBC provided constituency services, "gathered and disseminated information, engaged in administrative oversight, articulated the interests of specialized groups within the black community (such as business and labor), and devolved legislative proposals."[22] For example, when black legislators met with Richard Nixon (after being denied a meeting with him for more than a year), they presented him with 61 recommendations for governmental action. At the meeting, the CBC proclaimed its representation on behalf of all blacks across the nation. Diggs, the first chairperson of the CBC (1969–71), declared, "Our concerns and obligations as members of Congress do not stop at the boundaries of our districts; our concerns are national and international in scope. We are petitioned daily by citizens living hundreds of miles from our districts who look on us as Congressman-at-large for black people and poor people in the United States."[23]

Following the initial founding and the leadership of Diggs came the election of Carl B. Stokes. Stokes brought a major change to the CBC. As he explained, "At first we were unclear about our proper role. Therefore, in the past year, we had to analyze what our resources were, what we should be doing, and how best to do it. And our conclusion was this: If we were to be effective, if we were going to make the meaningful contribution to minority citizens in this country, then it must be as legislators. This is the area in which we must possess expertise—and it is within the halls of Congress that we must make this expertise felt."[24]

Throughout the years, the CBC has positioned itself to play a prominent role in Congress. Today, it has expanded beyond its primary legislative functions to include a foundation that focuses on community outreach. Since its founding the CBC has faced questions about its effectiveness and, with the election of Barack Obama, relevance in advancing the agenda of blacks. However, most people associated with the caucus recognize its importance in the legislative process, as many similar caucuses have developed in the state legislatures.

State Legislative Black Caucuses

State legislative black caucuses, beginning as informal groups and transitioning into formal organizations, proliferated from the 1950s through the 1980s. Before the Voting Rights Act of 1965, black elected officials serving in the state legislatures were few and far between.[25] With the implementation of the VRA, the number of black legislators increased dramatically. Along with other social and political conditions, the rise in the number of black state legislators enabled the proliferation of black caucuses throughout the states. For example, the Virginia Legislative Black Caucus was established due to "a surge in the size of the black delegation in 1985, and revitalization of the Virginia Association of Black Elected Officials—after being inactive for 16 years," with the express purpose "of institutionalizing the articulation and promotion of black political interests in Virginia."[26] Similarly, the Georgia Legislative Black Caucus was established to help black legislators handle "the volume and complexity of legislation and the lack of support staff; . . . to negotiate with the governor and legislative leaders to pass legislation beneficial to blacks; and finally, to develop a community outreach program to interact with the collective members' constituencies."[27] Additionally, many other state black caucuses organized due to the lack of symbolic and substantive policy responsiveness by white legislators. Overall, black caucuses represent the best organized and historically the strongest of the nonparty groups. Most of the organizations have existed since the 1970s, when voters elected black members to state legislatures in mass numbers for the first time following Reconstruction.

Formal state black caucuses exist in at least 30 states; 2 of these are general minority (Rhode Island) or black and Hispanic (Wisconsin) groups. The geographic dispersion of black caucuses offers few surprises, with 80 percent of the organizations existing in states with the largest black populations. Along the same lines, all 16 states in which blacks make up more than

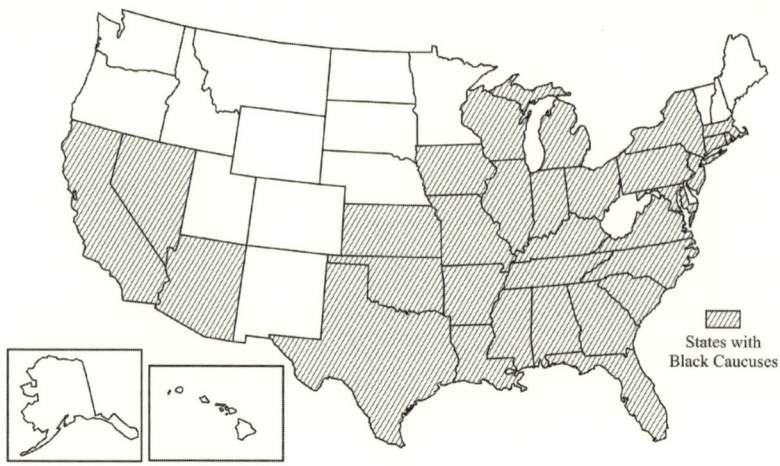

FIGURE 2.1. States with Legislative Black Caucuses

10 percent of the legislature have black caucuses; states in the Deep South make up nearly a third of the organizations. On the other hand, the Iowa Black Caucus is often made up of a single legislator, and only 10 blacks have ever been elected to the statehouse; however, the organization exists (when a black legislator is in office) as an offshoot of the National Black Caucus of State Legislators.

One unifying and organizing factor for the caucuses is the existence of the National Black Caucus of State Legislators. Founded in 1977, the organization offers membership, research services, and a national committee structure (e.g., national committees on housing and postsecondary education) to all black legislators and has members from across the country, including from states that do not have a black legislative caucus. The national organization runs the groups of at least two states (Iowa and Oklahoma). Another unifying factor is the black caucuses' de facto partisanship. Between 1999 and 2002, in the 27 states with formal black caucuses, there were only two Republican members (1 each in Missouri and New Jersey), which allowed the caucuses to focus their legislative agenda within the Democratic Party.[28]

The aims of the legislative black caucuses differ slightly from state to state. The goals of some of the caucuses are to specialize, negotiate, and reach out; others want to directly affect legislation; and yet others exist primarily to provide a forum for discussion and to inform citizens of political activity. For example, the South Carolina Legislative Black Caucus tries to work "exclusively for the promotion of the common good and general welfare of the people who look to [its] cooperation for guidance and leadership."[29] The Missouri Legislative Black Caucus seeks to influence state legislation, policy, and programs by working with all branches of government, as well as to conduct research and develop plans to increase the caucus's effectiveness in representing all Missourians.[30] Despite variation in the specific goals of the state black caucuses, they share the principal objective of passing legislation that is in the best interests of blacks.

In terms of membership, state legislative black caucuses have become increasingly more inclusive of potential members. Georgia, North Carolina, Mississippi, Missouri, and South Carolina opened membership up to all members of their legislatures, regardless of color and party identification, the only condition being that members must possess and work toward the ideals and principles established in the caucuses' by-laws. Virginia remains the only state with a black caucus that is both formally partisan and racially exclusive. Overall, the black caucuses across the country share similar backgrounds and purposes, represent comparable types of districts, have members with similar backgrounds, and struggle toward related legislative goals.

The Institutionalization of the Louisiana Legislative Black Caucus

Long before the LLBC was formally organized in 1977, blacks first played a role in Louisiana politics at the state's constitutional convention in New Orleans on November 23, 1867. Slaves had been considered free since the passing of the Emancipation Proclamation in 1863, but the overwhelming majority of white southerners did not accept the fundamental idea that blacks were equal to whites. Thus, Louisiana and the other southern states passed laws to control the freedoms of former slaves. Indeed, in 1865, slave codes were authorized by the Louisiana legislature, which severely restricted the movement and aspirations of blacks, especially with respect to their role in government.

Nonetheless, 49 black delegates were elected to the state's constitutional convention. Many of these delegates were biracial (part French) and in their twenties and thirties. The delegates were "unified both economically and politically," and together "they represented much of the political experience and wealth of the black population. Many of them were business leaders, some had the highest paying professions, and their educational training was above average for their race and was, at least, equal to that of the white delegates."[31] Their backgrounds were in business, the military, the ministry, education, and other professions. The delegates' qualifications proved to white legislators that they functioned as leading members of society and could be effective delegates.

At the convention, black delegates took an active part in committee deliberations. They were assigned to groups such as the Committee on Rules and Regulations (with 5 black members), the Committee on Militia (with 7 black members, including Pinckney Benton Stewart Pinchback, who chaired the committee), the Committee on Public Education (4), and the Committee to Draft a Bill of Rights (5).[32] The impact of black legislators was evident in the passage of the state's constitution. The major issue facing the state and the convention was that of equal rights. Black legislators advocated for universal suffrage and equal rights. Pinchback introduced an article to the Louisiana Constitution addressing civil rights, in which he argued that blacks should receive the "same rights and privileges as whites on common carriers and in places."[33] The Committee on Revision accepted the following as Article 13: "All persons shall enjoy equal rights and privileges upon any conveyance of a public character; and all places of business for which a license is required by either State, parish or municipal authority, shall be deemed places of a public character and shall be opened to the accommodation and patronage of all persons, without distinction or discrimination on account of race or color."[34]

On March 9, 1868, the delegates adopted the constitution by a vote of 71 to 6. The new document provided many equal rights for blacks, including state citizenship, voting rights, and integrated public schools.[35] Of course, there were some whites, even among those voting in favor of the constitution during the legislative process, who hoped that it would not be ratified. Nevertheless, in April 1868 the voters ratified the Louisiana Constitution, with more than 57 percent supporting it.[36]

Directly following the ratification of the constitution, the state held general elections, and for the first time blacks were elected to Congress, the state legislature, and other statewide offices. Charles E. Nash, a former sergeant in the Union army, was elected in 1875, the first black to represent Louisiana in the U.S. House of Representatives. Pinchback was elected to the U.S. House in 1874 and then to the Senate in 1876; however, he never served, because white Democrats disputed the election results and put their own candidates in office. C. C. Antoine became the lieutenant governor in 1872 and served until 1876. Lastly, Antoine Dubuclet served as state treasurer from 1868 to 1878.

In the years 1868–76 a total of 97 black representatives and 24 black senators served in the state legislature. The number of blacks serving in the legislature fluctuated from 28 to 36 in the house and from 7 to 15 in the senate. During this period of political influence, black legislators pushed their agendas, such as civil rights and education issues. They also proposed bills for personal gain, and "at least three Representatives and 2 Senators secured legislation giving them ferry privilege in their districts."[37]

Although blacks were relatively successful in the legislature from 1868 to 1876, the Compromise of 1877 erased the progress that blacks had made. In the legislature, the number of black representatives was reduced to 2 and the number of black senators to 1. The agreement negotiated between the North and the South stated that "in return for southern support of the Union, an acceptance of national supremacy, and an agreement to allow [Rutherford B.] Hayes to assume the presidency without a majority of votes, the national government agreed to end military occupation of the South, to cease its efforts at arranging southern society, and to lend tacit approval to white supremacy in the South."[38]

Acting as an enabler through its rulings, the Supreme Court facilitated the unequal treatment of blacks in the South. For example, in *Hall v. De Cuir* (1877) the Supreme Court found that the Louisiana statute allowing nonsegregated seating was an "unconstitutional invasion by a state of the federal government's exclusive jurisdiction over interstate commerce."[39] The Court also declared the Civil Rights Act of 1875 unconstitutional. Furthermore, President Hayes, honoring his part of the compromise, left the South to manage its own affairs. The end of Reconstruction brought the end of this brief period of black political prosperity. In the following four decades, "the state, local, and federal governments would serve as instruments of black subordination in the South."[40] The political impact of the federal government's negligence was overwhelming: no black served in the Louisiana legislature from 1879 until 1968.

Improvement in blacks' electoral success came with the passage of the 1965 Voting Rights Act. Section 2 of the act called for an end to racial discrimination by prohibiting voting practices or procedures that discriminated on the basis of race or color. While the passage of the VRA was critical, the federal government had a difficult time enforcing it. Nevertheless, the new law eventually catalyzed the increase in the election of blacks throughout the country. Since the implementation of the Voting Rights Act, roughly 200 blacks have served in the Louisiana legislature.

Although blacks have never served in the legislature at the high rate seen during Reconstruction, nor held a statewide office since Reconstruction, the improvement in blacks' electoral success cannot be overlooked. In 1968 Ernest N. "Dutch" Morial, of New Orleans, was the first black candidate elected to the Louisiana House of Representatives in the twentieth century. In addition to his achievement as the first modern black Louisiana representative, Morial was the first black to graduate from the Louisiana State University Law School; the first to become mayor of New Orleans; the first to be appointed a juvenile court judge; and the first to be elected to Louisiana's Fourth Circuit Court of Appeals, in 1974.

Morial was appointed to serve as a judge on the New Orleans Juvenile Court in 1970, and Dorothy Mae Taylor was elected as Louisiana's first black female legislator in 1971, serving until 1980. In 1983, she was appointed secretary of urban affairs by Governor Edwin Edwards. Finally, in 1986, Taylor was elected to the New Orleans City Council.

In 1974 Sidney John Barthelemy, who would serve as mayor of New Orleans from 1986 to 1994, became the first black Louisiana state senator since Reconstruction. Barthelemy also served two terms on the New Orleans City Council. The initial electoral victories of Morial, Taylor, Barthelemy, and others gave other black candidates hope, and subsequently more blacks have not only run but won.

In 1977, as the arrival of more blacks in the house presented an opportunity to form a formal caucus, ten individuals—Avery Alexander, Diana Bajoie, Sidney Barthelemy, Louis Charbonnet III, Nick Connor, Joseph

Delpit, Alphonse Jackson, Johnny Jackson Jr., Thomas Jasper, and Richard Turnley Jr.—led the founding of the Louisiana Legislative Black Caucus. Their goals were the following:

1. To provide equal opportunities for all blacks
2. To assist blacks in recognizing the need to repeal, enact, or reenact laws affecting their lives
3. To strengthen black economic development
4. To intercede and bridge the communication gap between government and blacks.[41]

In addition, a founding member of the LLBC explained that the caucus functioned to remind white legislators (who at the time represented districts with considerable black populations) that if they did not represent the interests of their black constituents, they would be held accountable in the next election.[42] In other words, the LLBC was an information source, keeping black constituents updated on whether white legislators supported or opposed their policy interests. In this sense, the caucus attempted to keep white legislators honest and active within the black community.

As discussed in detail in the next chapter, the LLBC has grown from its original 10 members in 1977 to more than 30 members during the first decade of the twenty-first century. However, a few key components have changed in the past thirty years. Most important is that most white members no longer represent districts with a considerable black population, as all 32 members of the LLBC represent majority-minority districts. The proliferation of these districts has allowed the LLBC to increase in size, but it has also removed one of the early functions of the caucus: holding white legislators accountable to their often sizable black constituencies.

Conclusion

Both the Congressional Black Caucus and state legislative black caucuses emerged to continue the struggle for political equality and favorable policy outputs, as did the black national conventions, black national political parties (such as the Freedom Now Party and the Peace and Freedom Party), black state political parties (such as the Mississippi Freedom Democratic

Party and the United Citizens Party of South Carolina), and protest organizations (such as the NAACP, the Urban League, and the SCLC) before them. Black caucuses became increasingly popular as more blacks were elected to state legislatures in the 1970s.

State black caucuses exhibit a strong, unified identity, both politically and socially. Most black caucus members are Democrats and male, although women are winning more elections; they are typically well educated, possessing college or postgraduate degrees, and usually work in education, business, or law. Districts represented by black legislators have predominantly black constituencies with high poverty rates and low levels of education. The similar identities of state legislative black caucuses are also evident in their general goals and policy initiatives. Their principal objectives are to achieve a better way of life for the black population in their state and to pass legislation that is in the best interests of blacks. Black caucuses provide black legislators with a forum for policy discussion through which they can inform black constituents of political activity in the legislature.

The black political struggle in Louisiana has been similar to those in other Deep South states, with a brief period of political prosperity during Reconstruction followed by a century of segregation and almost complete separation from the political system. However, over the past 30 years many states have seen the establishment and growth of caucuses like the LLBC to help solidify blacks' ability to represent their constituents and the greater black community.

3

Views from the Louisiana Legislative Black Caucus

> For so many years we were individuals without a voice and no one was looking out for blacks in the state of Louisiana, and you were only getting the crumbs from the table.... With the LLBC, our members are out there fighting for the poor people—particularly for the black people in the state that have been without a voice and disenfranchised.
> —LLBC member

> Because of the existing attitudes and mindsets that don't necessarily favor the minority and the black community, the Black Caucus is a presence in the legislature fighting for the minority community.
> —LLBC member

From the members' perspectives, the importance of the Louisiana Legislative Black Caucus is unquestionable. Yet, while the organization has been around for more than 30 years, the members often work in relative obscurity in the ornate halls of the Louisiana State Capitol as they strive to represent their constituents. How do they fight for the minority community and try to bring more than crumbs to their constituents? In this chapter we examine the legislative context within which LLBC members generally operate, as well as offer profiles of LLBC members and their districts. To tell the story of the LLBC, we focus on questions regarding the delegates' ideologies, income levels, important policy issues, attitudes toward a range of national black leaders, personal racial identities, and views of representation.

Much of what we know about black legislative life comes from a series of studies led by James Button and David Hedge.[1] Drawing on nationwide surveys from 1991–92, Button and Hedge show similarities between white and black legislators in terms of educational background and other demographics, as well as their views of politics and governing. The key differences they highlight involve how the legislators perceive the quality of life of black legislators and race relations in the legislature. They focus specifically on black legislators' perceptions concerning the quality of their legislative life and find that the more senior members, males, those who represent majority white districts, and those who represent more affluent districts are more likely to report better race relations and to have a more positive legislative experience.[2] Additionally, they find little evidence to suggest that as the percentage of blacks in the legislature has increased, particularly in the Deep South states of Louisiana and Mississippi, black members have expected to "be in any better position to form working coalitions with white Democrats."[3]

From this broader context, we move to our analysis of Louisiana legislative life in 2005 and 2006. We expect to find, as Button and Hedge did, that black and white legislators had similar backgrounds. In examining legislative life and job satisfaction, we take a slightly different approach, focusing on issues of racial identity and representational roles. However, we do expect to find some similar issues and concerns among the black legislators in regard to their ability to work with white legislators in order to form coalitions, garner attention for their agendas, and gain leadership roles within the chambers.

Inside the Louisiana General Assembly

The political culture of Louisiana is very different from that of other states. Observers often view Louisiana politics as a "gumbo," a favorite food of the people of Louisiana, which is a stew made from a conglomeration of local ingredients. Wayne Parent captures the uniqueness of Louisiana politics in the following observation:

> The differences between Louisiana and all of the other states are legion. No other state has a French-based legal system. No other state has an election system where two Democrats and two Republicans can face each other in the final vote on general election day. No

other state has had as many constitutions. No other state has such a curiously powerful governor with such curiously weak constitutional prerogatives. Add these and other features to a perhaps unparalleled record of political corruption and the end result is a state that can claim itself systematically, objectively, scientifically unique.[4]

The governor wields a great deal of power, yet that power does not rest in the constitution; instead, "the basis of a governor's power [has] almost always [been] political patronage—handing out jobs and pet projects for votes."[5] The Democratic Party has traditionally dominated the legislature, and the "existence of New Orleans, in short, makes Democrats much more competitive in Louisiana than in the other states in the Deep South."[6] As figure 3.1 illustrates, from 1980 to 2004 Democrats ruled both the senate and the house in Louisiana; however, as in most southern states, this dominance has diminished, with the Republicans coming within two seats (with three independents) of the Democratic majority in the house following the 2007 elections.[7] However, Louisiana Democrats are not the quintessential "New York Democrats"; they are "Southern Democrats," with a much more conservative ideology.

Despite Democratic control in both chambers, the one-party dominance has not produced "signs of party organization or cohesion." For example, as Parent writes, "Republicans and Democrats alike hold top positions of leadership in both chambers, and neither party can claim any semblance of discipline, even on procedural votes."[8] Further, even though Democrats are in the majority, some of the committees are chaired by Republicans. In the 2004, 2005, and 2006 legislative sessions, Republicans (who were in the minority) either chaired or made up the majority in the following committees: Transportation, Highways, and Public Works (majority); Insurance (majority); House Governmental Affairs (chaired); Judiciary (chaired); Administration of Criminal Justice (chaired); Commerce (majority); Education (chaired); and Retirement (chaired).

Due to the lack of institutional party strength, interest groups are a powerful force in the Louisiana legislature. According to one member, at one point lobbyists could go directly onto the floor of the chamber during debate, and often they would even vote for legislators. However, their unfettered access to legislators was changed due to corruption and scan-

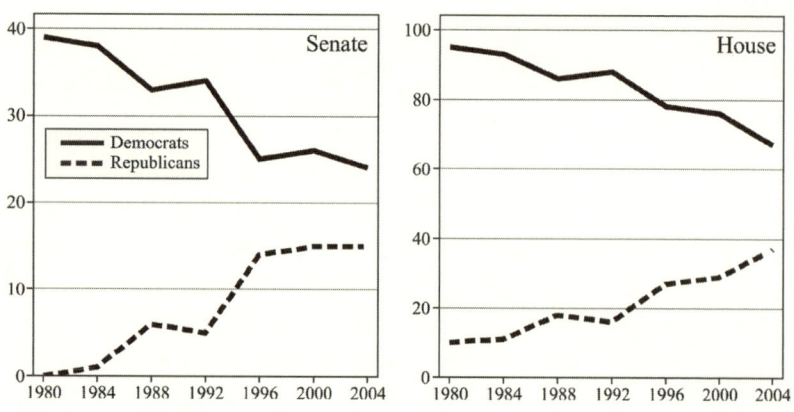

FIGURE 3.1. Louisiana Legislators by Party, 1980–2004. Adapted from R. Haynie, *Louisiana Legislature*.

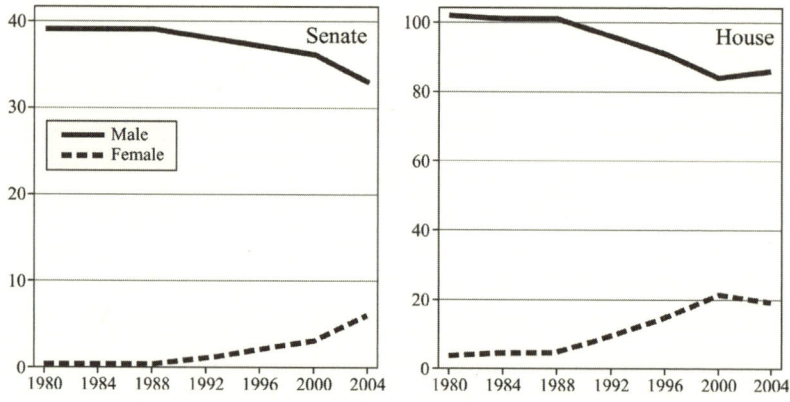

FIGURE 3.2. Louisiana Legislators by Gender, 1980–2004. Adapted from R. Haynie, *Louisiana Legislature*.

dals. Nonetheless, with only a small gold railing separating them from the legislators, the lobbyists' presence still lingers on the floor of the chamber.[9]

Men dominate the legislature, as figure 3.2 shows. However, women are an ever-growing sector. Although the first female senator was not elected until 1992, by 2004 there were six women serving in the state senate. Likewise, the election of female representatives has also increased since 1992, when there were nine women serving in the house; by 2004 the number had doubled.

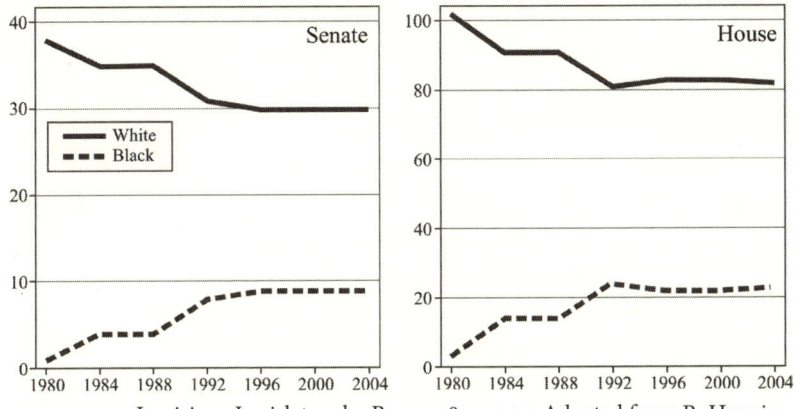

FIGURE 3.3. Louisiana Legislators by Race, 1980–2004. Adapted from R. Haynie, *Louisiana Legislature*.

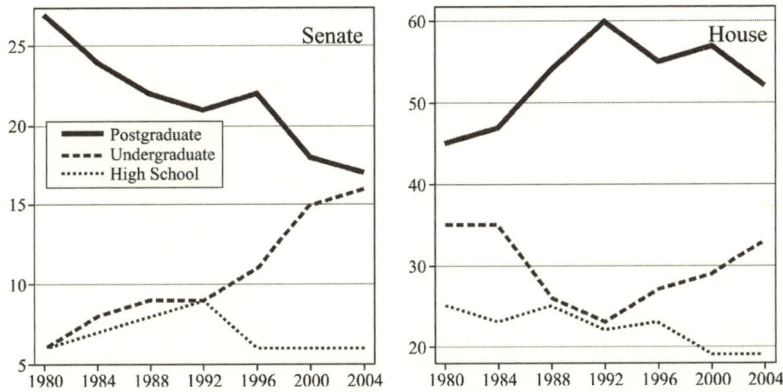

FIGURE 3.4. Louisiana Legislators by Education Level, 1980–2004. Adapted from R. Haynie, *Louisiana Legislature*.

The racial composition of the legislature is overwhelmingly white, as shown in figure 3.3. As of 2004 there were 32 black delegates in the Louisiana legislature: 9 representatives and 23 senators. The 1990 redistricting led to a substantial increase in the number of black legislators because black candidates were able to win elections in heterogeneous, majority-minority districts.

Louisiana's legislature is for the most part highly educated (see fig. 3.4). A majority of the members have earned either a college or postgraduate degree. As of 2004, however, 19 representatives and 6 senators had only a high-school diploma. Nonetheless, what figure 3.4 does not show is that many of the legislators lacking college degrees were attending college in Baton Rouge at the time, either at Louisiana State University (LSU) or Southern University. Furthermore, of those members with college degrees, senators were more likely to have attended and graduated from LSU or Southern, while house members were more likely to have attended and graduated from LSU, Loyola University, or Southern.

The majority of Louisiana legislators are employed outside the legislature; only a small number are full-time legislators. Most legislators work in business or law. Within the last decade or so, the number of attorneys has declined, particularly in the senate. The drop is "due in large part to a decrease in the number of 'country lawyers' from the North Louisiana and Acadiana areas and many of these seats have been transferred into the hands of members of the business-oriented professions."[10]

Profile of Louisiana's Black Legislators and Their Districts

Districts represented by members of the LLBC share many characteristics. In the 2005 and 2006 legislative sessions, the caucus had 32 black legislators, 23 in the house and 9 in the senate. All 32 members represented majority-black constituencies. The population of the average house district was 70.47 percent black, while the population of the average senate district was 63.4 percent black. Constituents in their districts were also relatively below average according to all socioeconomic indicators; for example, they typically had low incomes and a low level of education.

The profiles of the members of the 2005–6 LLBC are similar to those of members of black caucuses in other states and also to those of white legislators in Louisiana. Men dominated the caucus, with 17 men to 6 women in the house but nearly equal numbers in the senate, 5 men to 4 women. A majority of the caucus members had a college education or professional degree, as well as a career outside the legislature, many being either attorneys or educators. In terms of religious affiliation, most of the members were Baptists, and a small number were Catholics.

In a change from previous decades, black legislators held a number of leadership positions during the 2005 and 2006 legislative sessions. The

TABLE 3.1. Committee Leadership of Black Members in the Louisiana House and Senate, 2005–2006

Legislator	Position	Committee
House		
Yvonne Dorsey	Speaker pro tempore	
Avon Honey	Vice-chair	Education
Michael Jackson	Vice-chair	Health and Welfare
Richard Gallot	Vice-chair	House and Governmental Affairs
Karen Carter	Chair	Insurance
Willie Hunter	Chair	Labor and Industrial Relations
Ernest Baylor	Chair	Municipal, Parochial, and Cultural Affairs
Wilfred Pierre	Chair	Natural Resources
Israel Curtis	Vice-chair	Retirement
Roy Quezaire	Chair	Transportation, Highways, and Public Works
Senate		
Sharon Broome	President pro tempore	
Donald Cravins	Vice-chair	Judiciary B
Lydia P. Jackson	Vice-chair	Judiciary C
Edwin Murray	Vice-chair	Labor and Industrial Relations
Cleo Fields	Chair	Local and Municipal Affairs
Ann Duplessis	Vice-chair	Local and Municipal Affairs
Charles Jones	Chair	Senate and Governmental Affairs

speaker pro tempore of the house was Yvonne Dorsey, and the president pro tempore of the senate was Sharon Weston Broome. (When Broome served in the house, she was the first black elected to the post of speaker pro tempore.) Table 3.1 provides a list of black members' committee leadership positions in the house and senate during the 2005 and 2006 sessions. Nine house members and 6 senators served as either chair or vice-chair of a committee. However, the committees they headed, which included the Education, Judiciary, Governmental Affairs, Transportation, and Local and Municipal Affairs Committees, tended to be the less powerful ones. While the Judiciary Committee is important and powerful in many states, black members rarely chair committees that allocate money, such as the Ways and Means and Appropriations Committees.

Ideology, Income, and Views on Policy and Black Leaders

In our surveys of LLBC members in the 2005–6 legislature, we asked each caucus member a series of questions regarding personal ideology, income, and views on important policy issues. Regarding ideology, of the 23 black legislators who responded to our survey, 10 considered themselves liberals; 12, moderates; and 1, conservative. With respect to annual income, 19 reported earning $70,000 or more. Respondents were asked to list the three public policy issues of greatest concern to them as legislators. The majority of members listed education first, health care second, and crime third. Additional policy issues mentioned in survey responses included the environment, war, and hurricane recovery.

LLBC members were asked to respond to statements or questions on a variety of other topics in order to gauge their overall political views. For example, on whether blacks should form their own party, 13 members responded no, while 10 said yes. On whether blacks should have control over the government in predominantly black communities, 21 either "strongly agreed" or "agreed," and 2 "disagreed." At the same time, however, on whether blacks should have their own nation, only 4 "agreed," while 19 "disagreed." On whether affirmative action (i.e., affirmative-action/equal-opportunity programs) was essential if inequalities were to be reduced, 22 "strongly agreed" or "agreed" that the policy was essential to reducing inequalities. On whether quotas failed to force employers to lower their hiring standards, 21 "strongly agreed" or "agreed." Finally, the question on which members' responses varied most was whether states should pass laws forbidding the burning of the American flag: 13 "strongly agreed" or "agreed," while 10 "disagreed" or "strongly disagreed." These responses provide a deeper understanding of the ideological diversity and policy differences between members of the caucus. Overall, members tended to agree more on issues traditionally related to the black community than on more general issues (table 3.2).

In addition to asking general profile questions, we wanted to gauge the LLBC members' feelings toward a variety of national black leaders. The survey included both black liberals and conservatives in order to determine whether there was a distinct preference for conservative or liberal black leaders. The legislators ranked leaders on a scale of 0–100 based on how

TABLE 3.2. Policy Attitudes among Black Legislators Serving in the Louisiana Legislature, 2005–2006

Policy Statement	Disagree No. (%)	Agree No. (%)
Blacks should form their own party.	13 (56.5)	10 (43.5)
Blacks should have control over the government in predominantly black communities.	2 (8.7)	21 (91.3)
Blacks should have their own nation.	19 (82.6)	4 (17.4)
Affirmative action (i.e., affirmative action/equal-opportunity programs) is essential if inequalities are to be reduced.	1 (4.3)	22 (95.7)
Quotas do not force employers to lower their hiring standards.	2 (8.7)	21 (91.3)
Should Louisiana pass laws forbidding the burning of the American flag?	10 (43.5)	13 (56.5)

favorably they viewed them (see table 3.3). Colin Powell scored highest, while Clarence Thomas scored lowest. Barack Obama (prepresidential days), Jesse Jackson, and Maxine Waters (California congresswoman) also had high favorability ratings, while lower ratings went to Louis Farrakhan, Mel Watt (North Carolina congressman), and Condoleezza Rice. Since half of the respondents were moderates, it is not surprising that they held Powell in such high regard, given his more moderate political reputation. The responses demonstrate that candidates at both ends of the ideological spectrum are viewed less favorably.

Racial Identity

Racial identity is a key psychological characteristic associated with minority groups, and we believe that a legislator's attitude toward racial identity can influence his or her policymaking decisions. The issue of racial identity has received a lot of attention from researchers. It has been shown to affect psychological function and policy preference.[11] For our purposes, policy preference is particularly relevant.

TABLE 3.3. Average Favorability of Black Leaders among Black Legislators

Black Leader	Average Favorability[a] ($n = 23$)
Colin Powell	83.5
Barack Obama	75.7
Maxine Waters	73.9
Jesse Jackson	69.8
Al Sharpton	64.8
Louis Farrakhan	59.9
Condoleezza Rice	53.1
Mel Watt	37.8
Clarence Thomas	19.5

[a]The scale ranged from 0 (least favorable) to 100 (most favorable).

Based on the findings summarized in table 3.4, it is clear that the LLBC members' perceptions of racial identity could influence their legislative decision making, particularly if those perceptions were inconsistent. In order to measure racial identity, we used the Multidimensional Model of Racial Identity (MMRI), a survey instrument created by Robert Sellers, Mia Smith, Nichole Shelton, Stephanie Rowley, and Tabbye Chavous.[12] The MMRI measures seven elements that make up a person's racial identity. In general, the survey results reveal little difference among respondents (see fig. 3.5). Specifically, almost no variation exists on the "private regard" scale, as most respondents expressed positive judgments about being black. Likewise, in the area of "centrality" most members admitted to having a "strong sense of belonging to black people." With a bit more variation on the "assimilationist" dimension, we find that most respondents felt that blacks should strive to be full members of the American political system. Overall, the black legislators demonstrated similar sentiments in these areas.

Respondents showed slightly more variation in their responses on the remaining four dimensions. On the "humanist" scale, the results show a slight leaning toward the idea that being an individual was more important than identifying oneself as black. On the "public regard" scale, respondents varied widely in their view of others' respect for black people. There was no

TABLE 3.4. Research on the Effects of Black Racial Identity on Policy Preferences

Source	Findings
Verba and Nie, *Participation in America* (1972)	Blacks participated at a higher rate in politics
Tate, *From Protest to Politics* (1993)	Increased black political interest and voter participation in Congressional elections and influenced opinions on affirmative action
Dawson, *Behind the Mule* (1994)	Influenced attitudes toward a range of policies
Kinder and Winter, "Exploring the Racial Divide" (2001)	Blacks supported social welfare programs
Dawson, *Black Vision* (2001)	Blacks supported economic nationalism, black feminist orientations and ideology, allowing more women to become members of the clergy

clear consensus among respondents concerning the "oppressed minority" scale or whether the racism blacks had experienced was similar to that of other minority groups. Finally, on the "nationalist" scale, we see an almost bimodal distribution concerning whether blacks would be better off adopting an Afrocentric view. Overall, legislators had similar feelings about being black and about the role of blacks in the political system, but they demonstrated greater variation in their opinions in other areas.

The results suggest that as with their backgrounds and ideological self-placement, LLBC members tended to be similar in terms of their values and their view of the world. As we shall see in chapter 6, these commonali-

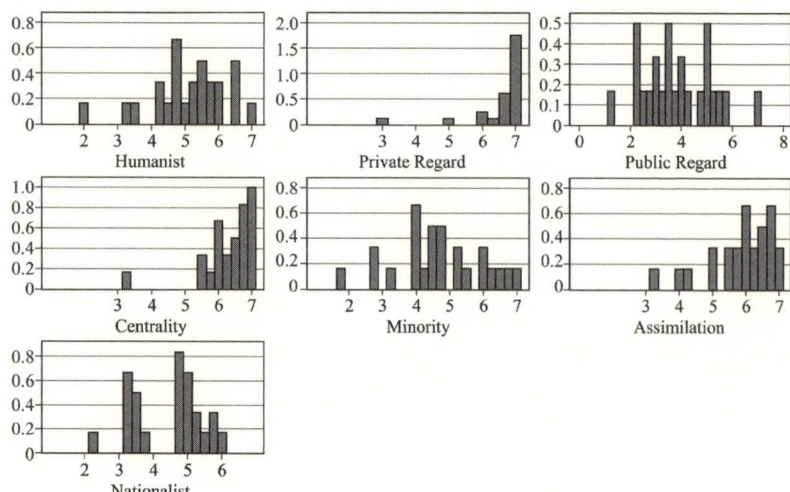

FIGURE 3.5. Louisiana Legislators' Self-Perceptions of Racial Identity. Each bar represents the percentage of respondents by rank (0–7 Likert scale) for each racial-identity question.

Source: Reproduced from Jas M. Sullivan and Jonathan Winburn, "Measuring the Effects of Black Identity on Legislative Voting Behavior: An Exploratory Study," *Journal of African American Studies,* 14 (2009), with the permission of Springer Science | Business Media.

ties, in addition to the same skin color or party label, help to explain why the LLBC is the most cohesive voting group in the Louisiana legislature.

Focus and Style

Legislative role theory is often used in the study of legislative behavior. As John Wahlke and his colleagues explained, the theory "yields a model of the legislature as an institutionalized human group which logically incorporates the model of the individual legislators to problems of legislative structure and function."[13] A legislative role is "a set of norms of behavior that a person in the position of legislator has internalized, which (consciously or unconsciously) guides that person's actual behavior."[14] There are two classes of role orientations that relate to legislative representation: the focus of representation and the style of representation.

Representational focus refers to the legislator's ideas concerning whom he or she ought to represent, as a representative can determine constituency in numerous ways. The three focus orientations are (1) district orientation, (2) state orientation, and (3) district and state orientation. In *district orientation,* the representative considers the district or county to be relevant in the conception of his or her job or emphasizes the district as a determining factor in his or her legislative behavior; in *state orientation,* the representative usually emphasizes the state above the district; and in *district and state orientation,* the representative places emphasis on both the district and the state.[15]

Representational style refers to the legislator's view of how he or she ought to represent constituents. Heinz Eulau and his colleagues distinguish three styles of representation: As *trustees,* representatives serve as free agents, making decisions based on their own judgment rather than on the specific views of their constituency. *Delegates* make decisions based on the views of their constituents even if they personally disagree. Finally, *politicos* behave in the manner of trustees on some issues and in the manner of delegates on others.[16]

Aside from the empirical studies conducted on general legislative role orientations, there has been only limited systematic research on the role perceptions of black legislators. In one study looking at the 102nd Congress, James Johnson and Philip Secret found that black members focused on the district and reflected a politico representational style.[17]

In order to discern the representational focus of the LLBC members, we used a survey instrument created by Johnson and Secret.[18] We made minor modifications to their survey questions, which were designed for use with black members of the U.S. Congress, in order to better fit our study of LLBC members. All statements regarding focus and style were presented in an "agree"/"disagree" format and measured on an 11-point scale, from 0 to 10. The three focus statements were:

1. "First and foremost, the job of a member of the state legislature is to represent his or her particular district, even before considering the interest of the state."
2. "When district/constituency needs conflict with the needs of the state, the legislator should put state interests first."
3. "Since state legislators are elected from districts, a legislator

should devote the bulk of his/her time to representing the interests of his or her particular district."

The three style statements were:

1. "Because the people seldom know all the aspects of important issues, a member of the state legislature serves all people best if he or she is left alone to make careful decisions by him or herself."
2. "If a legislator does not know his or her constituents' desires on a particular issue, it is his or her job to seek out constituency opinion before taking a stand on that issue."
3. "A member of the state legislature can vote correctly on most issues by asking himself or herself if the bill is the right thing to do."

In evaluating the survey results, we analyzed both individual items within the focus and style categories and composite scores for each of these categories. Figure 3.6 presents the frequency distribution for each of the three focus statements. For statement 1, the mean score was 8.48, indicating that black legislators agreed that they should represent the district before considering the interests of the state. Nearly 90 percent of LLBC members scored as moderately to very strongly in favor of the district focus, while two black legislators scored as strongly favoring the state focus. The overall distribution for statement 1 shows a predominant consensus toward the district orientation. On statement 2, LLBC members fell slightly to the district side, with a mean score of 5.35. On statement 3, there was a moderate to high district orientation among members. With a mean score of 8.43 and only one member in disagreement, the legislators indicated that they should spend the bulk of their time on district needs. From these findings, we see a strong focus on representing district interests and spending time in the district. However, when there is conflict between state and district interests, we see a slight variability in the answers. Nevertheless, the overall focus-scale score (the three focus statements combined to form a single factor) indicates a moderate to strong district orientation among LLBC members (mean = 7.42).

Turning to style, figure 3.7 highlights the frequency distribution for each of the three style statements. For statement 1, the mean score was 4.04,

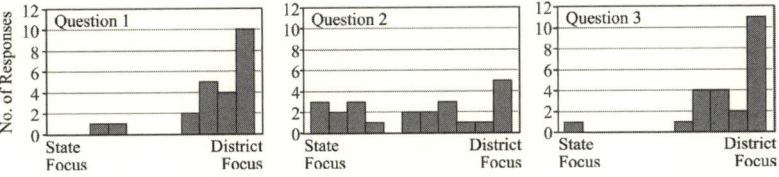

FIGURE 3.6. Representational Focus of LLBC Members

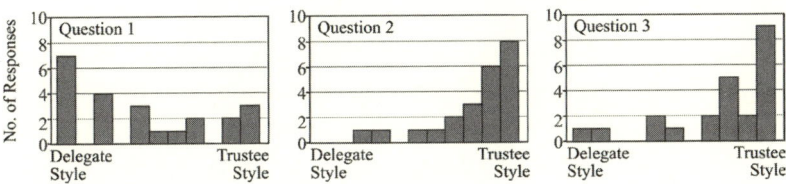

FIGURE 3.7. Representational Style of LLBC Members

indicating that LLBC members tended to lean toward a delegate position, believing that a state legislator serves the people best by taking cues from his or her constituency rather than making decisions on his or her own. On style statement 2, LLBC members possessed moderate to high trustee orientation (mean = 8.17), reflecting the opinion that if a legislator did not know his or her constituents' desires on a particular issue, it was not the legislator's job to seek out constituency opinion before taking a stand on that issue. On statement 3, there was a moderately high trustee orientation (mean = 7.65), reflecting the opinion that a member of the state legislature could vote correctly on the basis of his or her own judgment.

The overall mean style-scale score was 6.62, indicating that LLBC members occupied the politico position on the spectrum. In the final analysis, these representational role types could influence not only legislative decision making but also the way in which legislators interact with their constituents.

Our survey results indicate that members of the LLBC saw themselves as district representatives first and foremost. While they demonstrated solidarity in their views toward racial identity and other factors, their legislative priorities were with their districts. Once again, black legislators in Louisiana and across the country represent majority-minority districts. Therefore, although they place the district first, they still focus on issues related to blacks, albeit with a concentration on their own constituencies.

Overall, members did not have a consistent view of their style of representation, as they appear to fit the definition of politicos, sometimes favoring a delegate model and other times favoring a trustee model. Thus, the LLBC members' general orientations toward representation were not very different from those of most legislators across the country.

A Deeper Insight through Interviews

We interviewed 20 LLBC members, from both the house and the senate, during the summer and fall of 2007. Members who agreed to participate met with us either in an office near their chamber or in the cloakroom. The interviews, in which we asked 18 questions, lasted about twenty minutes and were tape-recorded with the members' permission. We informed the interviewees that we would not disclose their identities.

We began the interviews by asking why the members had run for legislative office. While their reasons varied to some degree, they all expressed the desire to "give back," "get things done," "effect change," and "represent black interests." On effecting change, one LLBC member stated, "We [blacks] have not been given the equal opportunity to have a true bite at the apple, and it's my job to make sure we get that living in Louisiana." Along the same lines, another LLBC member gave a couple of reasons for running: "First, I never saw people in the legislature that looked like me, so I wanted to enter into that arena to effect change; in addition, the area I ran for office is a high-poverty area, and individuals in the district knew we didn't have representation for a long time. I ran because people in the community asked that I run for public office, so changes could be made in the district." Many wanted to be part of a solution and had not run for personal reasons. In the voices of the LLBC members there was an undeniable tone of disheartenment at the fact that their community had remained in a vicious cycle of poverty one legislative session after another.

Next, we asked the LLBC members to define the most pressing needs of their districts. Not surprisingly, most said that their districts faced high levels of poverty and crime, poor education and health care, and a lack of economic development. One LLBC member explained, "We all face the same challenges in terms of job creation, job retention, education, and trying to deal with the high numbers of drop-out rates in our schools."

Another member said, "The two focal points that need to be addressed are crime and education. I think we cannot overly emphasize the importance of education and making sure that our children get educated, because that is the only way they will excel within in their community." Several members also mentioned the need for basic necessities. "The most pressing needs in my community are the availability of basic necessities that people require for their daily livelihood, such as grocery stores, restaurants, and things that really improve the quality of life." In addition, many noted that white elected leaders had lost sight of the importance of the black community. As one LLBC member put it, "Local elected leaders in the New Orleans area have to realize the value of my community and start developing more business and services for the people who live there." In essence, members not only were clearly aware of the problems confronting their community but had ideas about how to fix them.

We also examined the need for the LLBC. As expected, there was unanimous consensus among the members regarding the importance of the caucus. In the words of one member, "Our needs in the legislature were not being met. We always felt that in numbers there's strength, and that's why there is a reason for the Black Caucus. In addition, through the Black Caucus, we can act together (as a team) in reaching out to blacks throughout the state, with similar goals to fixing the shared problems." Another LLBC member stated, "There are issues common to black folks (including poor folks) that can be changed if we act together. Historically, the Black Caucus has been the voice for the voiceless. For example, in St. Tammany Parish, out of eleven judgeships, none are black. The Black Caucus put together a bill that created a minority district within the Parish that could get a black judge on that court. So, we try to provide assistance for those who need our help."

Some members indicated that in addition to being the voice of blacks and the poor, the LLBC was needed to help pass legislation. As one member pointed out, "You have such a small group, and if we don't unite and work together, and support one another, then we won't be able to accomplish our goals." All of the LLBC members viewed the caucus as necessary.

We asked LLBC members to tell us how the caucus served them personally. Some noted that it served as an informational and educational source. One member said that "it serves as an opportunity to collaborate. It serves as an opportunity to share with people who have to deal with similar problems in their districts that I have to. In this respect, it gives us an opportunity to strategize on how to deal with improving our districts." Some also noted that the caucus served to obtain support for members' policies. As one member stated, "The Black Caucus supports me in legislation. Sometimes I feel that if it hadn't been for the Caucus, I would not have gotten a bill out of committee. We support one another in getting legislation passed." This opinion was shared by other LLBC members.

While all of the LLBC members believed that the caucus was necessary and served vital functions, many admitted that members did not see eye-to-eye on all issues. Some members were not willing to shed light on the in-house fighting; however, other members were a little more open. Most members indicated that while there was usually agreement in the caucus concerning policy issues, this was not always the case in other areas. "I agree about 70 percent of the time with the Black Caucus," one interviewee told us, "because with some of the issues, I see a different perspective. Majority of the time, I do agree that some issues can be dealt with differently. I think that more strategy should be used in terms of how to leverage and how to get things done, and sometimes I see that decisions are made hastily and not well thought out. In addition, sometimes there is a conflict of ego."

Nonetheless, most of the members indicated that they agreed with the caucus 90–100 percent of the time. The rationale for their overwhelming support of the caucus was that it would benefit their constituents. It was very clear that members were mindful of their purpose in the legislature. One member explained, "I agree with the members of the Caucus 100 percent of time because I just know it's the right thing to do. The members are fighting for the kinds of things that impact the people in our community in a positive manner, and when we stand strong, as a whole, we can create change."

When we asked members to name the areas of most disagreement among LLBC members, there were some interesting responses. While some said that they could recall no particular areas of difference, others indicated that there certainly were areas of disagreement. A member of the first group responded, "I really can't pinpoint any overall areas that we disagree on. There may be bills that deal with local issues that members may not agree on, but I think on most occasions, we just agree on everything. We don't really have any problems as a group."

It was our impression that caucus members tended to disagree on issues related to morality. "One issue I think that we find most disagreement has been around the issue of life and the conception of when life actually starts," one member told us. "I think there's no agreement, really, in that area." Disagreements also arose among members whose districts were not completely black, even though all members represented districts with a black majority. Another member explained, "My particular district is mixed, and sometimes I have to find a way to represent the entirety in that district. Sometimes that puts me in a place where I might not be totally in line with what the Caucus has in mind on an issue." Thus, policy disagreements among caucus members may be rare, but they do occur.

Public policy is not the only area of disagreement. Some differences have to do with issues of power, for example. One member explained: "I guess disagreements would be in how we share power or how to wield power. You have to realize that not only are we African Americans and Black Caucus members, but we are human beings too, so we suffer from the frailties of egos and idiosyncrasies. So we have problems in the area of leadership and the direction of the leadership." Another member commented on the fact that some members were unwilling to admit that there might be more than one way of thinking about an issue: "Sometimes our disagreements come from different pieces of legislation. In the past, I was in favor of doing a bill on school vouchers, and the rest of the Caucus was against it. Well, my reasoning in supporting vouchers is to support children and families, but certain people hear certain words and they throw up barricades, and sometimes they don't take the time to understand how it could be positive."

Other areas of disagreement among LLBC members stem from conflicting interests between urban and rural areas and between the city of New Orleans and the rest of the state. As one member pointed out, "Historically, the majority of the Caucus has been New Orleans based, and they have really driven the agenda and had more of a voice in the Caucus. Sometimes, this causes members to forget about issues outside of New Orleans." On the conflict between urban and rural areas, another member explained, "There exist disagreements among urban and rural legislators. Your big metropolitan-area legislators quite naturally have an overall different perspective than a legislator who represents a rural community. So, areas of disagreements are divided between rural and urban legislators."

Concerning the policy process, we asked the LLBC members how the caucus helped them pass legislation. Interviewees responded that the support of the caucus was often enough to get a bill passed in the legislature. One member told us, "The Black Caucus helps you get legislation passed; you very well know there are twenty-something votes that you ordinarily will have based on common interests. But at the same time, the Caucus members can also act in getting you other votes based on the relationships they have with non–Black Caucus members." Another member explained the steps the caucus followed to ensure maximum support among its members before a bill even went through the committee process:

> We go over each member's piece of legislation. Members who offer the legislation share with the Caucus the specifics of the legislation and ask the Caucus for their support. From there, the Caucus members will either state whether they will support it or not support it in the present form. If there isn't a great deal of support, members will iron out the kinks to make it more acceptable for maximum Caucus support. Once that's achieved, it moves onto the legislative process.

Not all policy moves along this path, however. While members may discuss their legislation with fellow caucus members, lack of support in the caucus does not mean that the legislation dies there. Members will move their legislation on to the legislative process without the caucus's support.

We were interested in finding out whether LLBC members faced any obstacles in passing their legislation because of their race. Many of those we interviewed admitted facing some difficulties in getting legislation passed. One member responded:

> Sure. There are some areas that African Americans are just considered not to have any influence in—some of the financial issues. If you look at the makeup of the committees, most of the people that you'll see having influence over money committees (i.e., Ways and Means and Appropriations) are all white males, and typically, the black members are on Education, Municipal and Local Affairs, and Criminal Justice Committees. So, committee structure is unequal.

Another member acknowledged a kind of superficiality among certain white legislators. "On the surface, everyone is very outgoing, outspoken, and very cordial. But I think there are certain individuals that have it in the back of their mind that this is a white-boy fraternity and we are intruding upon their fraternity. However, this sentiment is held among a small minority. So for me, as a legislator, I don't worry about that. I just try to move good legislation forward to help all people."

LLBC members also stated that they faced obstacles in passing legislation dealing with minority-specific issues. "You always face obstacles when a piece of legislation pertains specifically to African American issues," one member told us. "For example, when legislation pertaining to sickle-cell anemia is offered, the support for it isn't always there among white legislators, because some people are not empathetic about it." Another member said that

> some folks have not yet been educated and sensitized to the fact that on some issues or public policy [others] may not be in the same persuasion as themselves. So, yeah, we are still constantly battling to defend, protect, and preserve on all issues. Racial prejudices still exist and it's unfortunate, but we handle it by not creating fear or talking down to our colleagues; however, we try to basically message, educate, and sensitize them by giving them facts and figures on the subject matter.

One the other hand, one LLBC member did not feel that he had personally faced any obstacles in passing legislation:

> I believe the ones that face the most opposition are the ones that always see every issue as either black or white, or they're up there pushing for black supremacy. So, I think those are the ones that pretty much have the most problems with facing obstacles. As for me, I will support the Black Caucus and black issues, but I will not be on the front end saying, I need this for black people. I'm not that type. It's the ones that are pro-black or those who overdo it [that] are the ones who face obstacles.

Since many LLBC members indicated that they faced some obstacles, we asked them what strategies they used to get their legislation passed.

Many of the members said that most often they started with the caucus. One member said simply, "Being a black legislator, I start with the Black Caucus." Another member told us, "I start with the Caucus, and I make sure they are aware of what's taking place. Then I move to members on the committee, so you know when it's coming to the House floor. You have to talk to the white members and make sure you get them, because if you don't get their help, then your bill won't pass." Many of the members acknowledged that they had to work with their white colleagues, and although they might start at the caucus level, they navigated the process by talking to members individually. One LLBC member said that his strategy began with the policy itself: "I start with the legislation itself. I want legislation that's out there to help all people. I don't particularly tailor it to any one social or economic group. I think that's important."

Another strategy members used to pass legislation was to form relationships with their colleagues. As one caucus member explained, "I start with my seat-mates, and the people that sit around me and build up their support. But one of the first things I do when I get here every day is walk the aisles and shake hands and talk to people. If I have a controversial piece of legislation, I put it out there to everyone before the committee meetings and let them ask me questions informally. Even if it is not controversial, I will follow the process of walking around and giving my colleagues an opportunity to ask me questions." Most members began with the caucus, but they also spoke with members of relevant committees and discussed their bills with individual members. Many of the legislators brought up the theme of building relationships and admitted that without certain relationships, success might be limited. Thus, members use a multipronged approach: they sought caucus support; they sought cosponsorship; they discussed their bills with members of the appropriate committees; and they built relationships with individual members.

Since many of the members relied on caucus support to pass legislation, we asked what the caucus's success rate was in passing legislation. Most of the LLBC members we interviewed agreed that the caucus had a high rate of success. One member said concerning the success of the LLBC:

> We had some measured success passing legislation. I think it could always be improved. However, when it [policy] deals directly with

Caucus issues, we have a higher rate. For example, the issue of voting rights for displaced New Orleans residents was a heated debate. We lost the first round of votes; however, we decided to engage in a silent protest by walking out on the legislature, which was very effective. We came back in and explained our position on the bill and ended up getting it passed. So depending on the issue, we're pretty good at getting things passed. When we are unified on a particular issue, we are tough to deal with.

However, others argued that the caucus could achieve a higher passage rate. "We're not as successful as we should be," said one LLBC member. "I believe in the last couple of years we have lost footing as opposed to gaining footing, in terms of what we are able to do. I don't know if we plan well enough. Part of it is that we don't have enough conversation about how to mobilize and move forward on great pieces of legislation that really impact the masses of people. This is a strategic mistake and that bothers me."

We also asked caucus members how they dealt with conflicting interests between the caucus and the Democratic Party. Specifically, we asked whether there had been an issue on which they had felt they had to side with the party rather than with the caucus. Most LLBC members responded that the interests of the caucus had rarely conflicted with those of the Democratic Party. However, many of the caucus members admitted that when there had been such an occasion, whether they sided with the party had depended on the issue. One member explained:

> It depends on the issue. I have no problem going against the Caucus, and I have done it in the past. The voting rights issue is a classic example. The Democratic Caucus opposed this issue and the LLBC supported it. All of the members of the LLBC broke ranks and voted to support the bill. In this respect, I'm not beholden to the LLBC or the Democratic Party. I try to represent my home district and 9 times out of 10, that's in line with the Caucus.

Chairs and vice-chairs of committees also support this line of thinking. One LLBC committee chairperson pointed out, "If the bill is supported by the party leadership, but it isn't beneficial to blacks in general, then I'm not supporting it. Even though I'm chairman, I'll go against the wishes of the party leadership." On the other hand, another LLBC committee vice-chair stated, "I have at times sided with the party leadership over the wishes of the Caucus. For example, when I looked at the bills as a whole, they may not have addressed as much as we wanted [as it relates to the Black Caucus], but in the end, it addressed a lot of the issues and concerns we had for our constituents. So, I supported the party leadership."

It is clear that party discipline is not strong; members seem to pick and choose which policies to support or oppose without any repercussions. We therefore asked LLBC members whether they thought there was a unified Democratic Party agenda. The majority of the LLBC members did not think there was. One veteran LLBC member explained, "I haven't seen it. I would say it's more of a Black Caucus agenda. The leadership of the Democratic Party needs a lot of work." Indeed, most members concurred that the LLBC had a clearer agenda and a stronger leadership than did the Democratic Party. Another member said that the LLBC agenda was "probably more unified" than that of the Democratic Party. "The major reason is that over the years, the Democratic Party was uncertain about who we are, and we haven't done a good job in defining and communicating who we are, because we have always been in the majority." Similar sentiments regarding the Democratic Party were expressed by most of the interviewees. For example, one LLBC member elaborated: "The Democratic Party has always been in the majority here, and there hasn't been a great emphasis placed on the party. However, now that the Republicans have gained in their numbers and have exercised their strength and ability to block certain legislation, it has forced the Democratic Party to come together and say if we don't start looking along party lines, we're going to get run over."

Our final question had to do with the LLBC members' overall experiences as legislators. Despite occasional frustrations, many of them enjoyed being a member of the Louisiana legislature. One member told us, "I love being able to assist people. I love being in a position where I can actually influence policy. But I have to tell you, some days I've gone home very frustrated at some of the logic that my colleagues use to support or oppose certain pieces of legislation. However, I come back another day, and those people you may not see eye to eye the previous day may be the person you have to work with in passing another piece of legislation. So, you can't be frustrated and angry for long." Another member said of his experience working to pass legislation that "it has taught me a lot about working in groups. In the House, I think it is group politics that commands. You have to be able to operate within a group, and so you have to, I think, work in a fashion that you don't alienate the members of any particular group, so you can get a broad support." All of the LLBC members we interviewed found joy in helping others, particularly ordinary constituents. As one member explained, "I'm able to go out and help kids get jobs here at the Capitol. When someone needs an internship at the Capitol, I do my very best to find them a slot. The bottom line is you're helping people. I'm not in this for myself. It's that you have an opportunity to help more people than before."

Conclusion

Our in-depth interviews and surveys demonstrate the multidimensionality of the LLBC members. We found that LLBC members shared not only similar district composition (majority black) but also personal characteristics, such as being highly educated and dedicated to their churches. In addition, most shared a similar ideology and similar views on black identity, and while black legislators are proud to be black, they are by no means Afrocentric. Their representational style is politico, and their representational focus is moderately to strongly district-oriented. The interviews revealed that while there is a great deal of consensus on policy issues and the need to improve the living conditions of blacks in Louisiana, there are still disagreements on how to achieve these. Although there are internal fights and divisions, members seem to be able to put aside their differences in order to work to benefit the greater black community.

In the remaining chapters, we empirically test several of the assertions and conclusions in this chapter. In particular, we examine whether LLBC members focus their agenda on issues related to the black community, whether they are able to pass legislation at rates similar to those of their white colleagues, and their overall voting cohesion. We show that the views of the members often accurately reflect the empirical reality. However, some of the conclusions we draw from our institutional-level analysis differ from those expressed by LLBC members here.

4

Setting the Agenda

In March 2006, following an acrimonious special session to deal with hurricane recovery, Senator Cleo Fields (D-Baton Rouge) summed up the LLBC's relations with the rest of the political system in the state as follows: "No permanent friends, no permanent enemies. Just issues."[1] He was repeating the Congressional Black Caucus's motto to describe the frustration of LLBC members as they tried to establish a policy agenda in the wake of Hurricane Katrina. As the group introduced their agenda for the 2006 regular session, they hoped to move beyond storm recovery and the restrictive agenda of their traditional ally, Democratic governor Kathleen Blanco. The group released a legislative packet heading into the 2006 regular session that outlined the 54 bills they considered most important. Their hope was to parlay some of the attention brought about by the hurricanes into areas the LLBC traditionally dealt with, such as affordable housing, in order to attract support for their policy proposals.

The initial phase of the legislative process, agenda setting or bill introduction, provides legislators the opportunity to express their views and represent specific constituency concerns.[2] As discussed in chapters 2 and 3, since blacks first entered the political arena following the civil rights movement, they have tried different ways to secure positive public policy and more legislative attention for black issues and black initiatives. Many LLBC members believe that the creation of the caucus and the increase in its membership have given blacks a chance to have their voice heard in the legislature. In this chapter, we examine whether there is indeed a difference between the agendas of LLBC members and those of the rest of the legislators, as well as whether race is a significant factor in members' agenda setting.

Background on Agenda Setting

When legislators head into session, setting an agenda is one of the most important aspects of their job, as it provides them with a foundation for pursuing their goals and representing their constituents. Within the legislature, introducing new legislation is the most direct way to put an agenda into practice. The process of introducing bills provides choices and alternatives for legislators to consider when attempting to alter public policy. Bill introductions also define whose alternatives the legislature considers, and they area direct mechanism by which legislators can meet their constituents' needs.[3]

Scholarly investigations consistently show that members' race does, in fact, influence the types of legislation they introduce.[4] Black legislators offer both substantive legislation (providing material goods and services to the black community) and symbolic legislation (entailing psychological rewards) that differs significantly from legislation offered by white members.[5] According to Kathleen Bratton and Kerry Haynie, "Race exerts a powerful influence on the introduction of black interest bills; black legislators introduce more black interest bills than do other legislators."[6] In the U.S. Congress, black members most often sponsored symbolic forms of

TABLE 4.1. Top Five Policy Areas of Legislation Introduced, by Group

Policy Area	LLBC		White Democrats		Republicans	
	Rank	% of Group Total	Rank	% of Group Total	Rank	% of Group Total
Appropriations	2	10.53%	1	15.72%	1	14.52%
Education	4	5.30	—		5	5.82
Health	—		5	6.71	—	
Law and Crime	3	10.19	3	8.67	3	9.89
State Government	1	14.27	2	10.47	2	11.69
Transportation	4	5.30	4	8.03	4	8.29

Note: The LLBC introduced 1,499 bills; the White Democrats, 2,314; and the Republicans, 1,942.

legislation, which did not "distribute or redistribute tangible benefits" to their constituents, but they do "confer symbolic recognition on groups."[7] Thus, research shows that race influences the types of bills introduced by legislators. In addition, it seems that the types of policies offered by black legislators differ from those offered by their white counterparts. Given this expectation, we start with a general look at the types of bills introduced by our three main groups, LLBC members, white Democrats, and Republicans (for an analysis of these groups, see the introduction).

Table 4.1 shows the top five policy areas on the 2005–6 agendas of these groups. Overall, we find very similar results across the three groups. Issues related to state government (primarily policies related to elections and government agencies); appropriations, revenue, and taxes; law and crime; and transportation dominated the agendas of all three groups. Legislation related to education made the top five for both LLBC members and Republicans, while health care rounded out the top five for the white Democrats. From this broad perspective, the agendas look quite similar. As the table shows, LLBC members did not propose agendas outside the mainstream of Louisiana politics. That is, they did not focus exclusively on civil rights or affirmative action and leave other policy issues to the white legislators. Broadly speaking, the LLBC had the potential for large-scale incorporation into the legislative process. However, this table only shows the general areas of policy priorities and does not tell us anything about the specifics of the agendas.

Analysis
Agenda Setting across the Three Groups

We know that the three major groups in the legislature focused on roughly the same issues, but how did their agendas relate to issues of concern to the black community? To examine this question, we coded for black-interest legislation.[8] Black-interest legislation covers areas of public policy often associated with the black community; these areas include, but are not limited to, issues of poverty, housing, and civil rights. In this chapter we use this coding to test for influences on the likelihood of introducing black-interest and race-specific legislation.

Our dependent variables are the number of black-interest and race-specific bills introduced. We analyze the total number of bills introduced by an individual legislator during the four sessions we studied. Given that bill introductions are count data and negatively skewed, ordinary least squares (OLS) regression is not appropriate. Rather, negative-binomial and Poisson-maximum-likelihood models are the two most common and appropriate count models.[9] Additionally, we cluster the models by individual to account for individual patterns across the four sessions. We present two models. In the first, our dependent variable counts black-interest legislation as the bills whose content is in substantive areas generally related to African Americans.[10] The second model is more specific: we only count bills that deal specifically with policy areas that are most traditionally related to blacks. This includes bills regarding civil rights, social welfare, and affirmative action. We code for these bills using a full text search measure.

While the first model takes into account areas traditionally related to blacks in a broad sense, the second model accounts for legislation that deals specifically with issues most closely associated with the black community. Overall, 16 percent of the introduced legislation dealt with black-interest legislation, while less than 2 percent dealt with the more specific racial issues. Across the four sessions, 95 percent of the legislators introduced at least one piece of general black-interest legislation, while just 29 percent introduced legislation more specifically related to blacks.

Our primary independent variables of interest focus on the race and party of the legislator. We have dummy variables for the three main categories—LLBC members, white Democrats, and Republicans. In the models, Republican is the base category with which we compare our results. We control for other potential explanatory variables that may influence the focus on black-interest legislation. Given the importance of New Orleans in Louisiana politics and the concentration of blacks in the population of New Orleans, we account for whether or not a member represented any part of Orleans Parish. New Orleans is also the main urban area in the state, which is important because the agendas of legislators representing Orleans Parish may have focused on urban problems that were often linked with black-interest issues regardless of their race.[11] Additionally, we account for the legislator's gender (0 = female, 1 = male), since women tend to introduce legislation that overlaps with traditional areas of black-interest social and economic policy.[12]

Additionally, we account for the total number of bills a member introduced during a session, as well as the percentage of resolutions a member introduced during a session. The total number of bills represents how active a member was during a session, while the percentage of resolutions represents a proxy for the time the legislator spent on symbolic representation. Given the importance of symbolic representation in studies of African American representation, we expect to find a positive relationship.

We also include institutional controls that may influence the bill-introduction process. These include seniority, leadership (both party and committee), and chamber. Since having seniority, holding a leadership position, and being in the smaller senate chamber are all factors that may lead to greater policy expertise and greater understanding of the legislative process, we control for these in order to account for differences in legislative experience. We code seniority as a member's total years in a chamber; leadership as "1" if the member was part of the chamber leadership and "0" if not; and chamber as "1" if the legislator was a member of the state senate and "0" if he or she was a member of the house.

We also examine environmental or district-level variables in the model. We do not include district demographics, since there are high levels of multicollinearity between the race of the representative and the demographics of the district represented. (The importance of district demographics is addressed in the next section.) However, we do include the percentage of the district population who were registered Democrats. Legislators, regardless of race, may be more likely to sponsor black-interest legislation due to the overlap between those issues and policy priorities of Democrats in general. Additionally, we include a measure of electoral safety, since members whose electoral position is safe may pursue a different agenda from that pursued by members who face a tough electoral situation.

Finally, we control for each individual session with a series of dummy variables. The 2005 regular session is our base category in the models. This is important, since we expect to find important differences between sessions given the timing of our study. The 2005 regular session was pre-Katrina, while the other three occurred in the immediate aftermath of the hurricane that forever changed New Orleans. Since there was an increase in attention to black-interest issues following the storm, we expect to find more black-interest issues on the agendas of the three sessions after the disaster.

TABLE 4.2. Likelihood of Introducing Black-Interest or Race-Specific Legislation

Variable	Model 1: Black-Interest Legislation[a]	Model 2: Race-Specific Legislation[b]
LLBC membership[c]	.5926 (.1663)***	1.438 (.4845)**
Republican Party membership[c]	-.142 (.1552)	-1.16 (.8024)
Orleans Caucus membership	.0315 (.1438)	.5368 (.3633)
Gender	-.299 (.1344)*	.2165 (.4566)
Seniority	-.017 (.0078)*	-.020 (.0289)
Party leadership	.4284 (.2435)	.038 (.7734)
Committee leadership	.2294 (.1227)	.2099 (.3085)
Chamber	-.129 (.1285)	.2284 (.3471)
Total introduced bills	.0473 (.0049)***	.0193 (.0072)**
% Resolutions	-.007 (.0022)***	.0062 (.0058)
Electoral safety	.0037 (.0025)	-.003 (.0071)
% district Democratic	-.013 (.0067)	-.052 (.0322)
2005 special session[d]	-.443 (.1652)**	-1.31 (.5080)**
2006 special session[d]	-.419 (.1790)*	-1.20 (.6391)
2006 regular session[d]	.005 (.1008)	.1891 (.2421)
Constant	.7976 (.4504)	.7211 (2.00)
α	.2523 (.0557)	
N	473	473
Log pseudo-likelihood	-732.84	-194.20

Note: Members who did not introduce legislation are excluded. Models are clustered by member. Each cell contains the coefficient estimate, with robust standard error in parentheses.

[a]Model 1: negative binomial regression.
[b]Model 2: Poisson regression.
[c]White Democrats are the base category.
[d]The 2005 regular session is the base category.

*$p < .05$, **$p < .01$, ***$p < .001$

Table 4.2 presents the relationship between introducing black-interest legislation and race-specific legislation and the independent variables discussed above. We find that LLBC membership is positively and significantly related to the introduction of black-interest and race-specific legislation. However, we do not find any other statistical relationships across the two models, except a positive influence for the total number of introduced bills and a greater focus on black-interest and race-specific legislation in the first special session than in the 2005 regular session. Somewhat surprising is the lack of significance of representing Orleans Parish, as well as the little difference between the 2006 and 2005 regular sessions. Given the potential post-Katrina effect, we hypothesized that more attention would be brought to historically black issues, which would increase the likelihood of introducing bills related to these issues. However, we do not find any evidence of such an effect. Part of any Katrina effect is captured by the special-session variables, as these sessions were called to deal specifically with post-hurricane issues.[13]

Looking at our control variables, we find that for members who introduced more bills, significantly more of those bills were related to black-interest issues. We also find that the percentage of resolutions a member introduced had a negative influence on the number of black-interest bills introduced; however, there was no significant relationship between the percentage of resolutions introduced and the number of race-specific bills introduced. The negative coefficient shows that members were more likely to introduce more black-interest legislation when they introduced fewer resolutions as a proportion of their overall agenda. This suggests that legislators are not more likely to deal with "black issues" from a symbolic rather than a substantive approach.

Given the properties of the count models, we cannot directly interpret the substance of these coefficients. For a better understanding of what these findings mean, we turn to predicted counts, or an estimation of the number of bills different members or groups of members would introduce in specific situations. In table 4.3 we present the predicted number of black-interest and race-specific bills that would be introduced across our three groups of interest, along with the percentage of change between groups. We hold all other variables at their appropriate means or modes, allowing us to compare the average legislators within our groups of interest. Given

TABLE 4.3. Predicted Number of Black-Interest and Race-Specific Bills Introduced, 2006 Regular Session

Group	Black-Interest		Race-Specific	
	Count	% Change	Count	% Change
LLBC	3.16	—	0.58	—
White Democrats	1.75	44.62	0.14	75.86
Republicans	1.52	51.90	0.04	93.10

Note: Count = the predicted number of bills introduced by a member of each group. % change = the percentage of change in the likelihood of bills introduced by LLBC members compared with the likelihood of bills introduced by White Democrats and Republicans.

the low likelihood of a black-interest or race-specific bill being introduced (the mean number of bills introduced per member is 2.95 and 0.37, respectively), the percentage of change provides a more substantively interesting discussion.

As we can see in table 4.3, for the more general coding of black-interest legislation we find that LLBC members are predicted to introduce 45 percent more black-interest bills than white Democrats and 52 percent more than Republicans. For race-specific legislation, we see a much larger influence, as members of the LLBC are predicted to introduce 76 percent more race-specific legislation than white Democrats and 93 percent more than Republicans. Overall, this shows that LLBC members were more likely to focus on general black issues and to introduce legislation dealing with more race-specific topics. Thus, while table 4.1 shows that the three groups introduced legislation on similar broad topics, when we look at the more specific focus of the legislation, there was variation across groups. Overall, black legislators are much more likely to introduce bills that relate to the black community.

Agenda Setting within the LLBC

It is not surprising that race is a significant predictor of the type of bills introduced in the legislature. Our findings concur with previous research (especially Kerry Haynie's *African American Legislators* [2001]), which shows that black legislators offer bills that are racial in nature and often differ from those of white legislators. However, we can go beyond these traditional findings by focusing specifically on differences between the agendas of LLBC members.

While "minority issues" did not appear directly as a top priority in our coding scheme (see table 4.1), it is clear from the above analysis that most members of the LLBC did focus part of their agendas on black-interest issues. Of the 32 LLBC members in the analysis, 31 introduced legislation on general black-interest issues, while 57 percent did not introduce any bills that fit into our race-specific category. While members of the LLBC have a common agenda based on broad issues that include black-interest areas, not all members specifically focus on race when they draft and introduce their agendas.

Part of the explanation for similar broad agendas is the similarity of the places black legislators represent. As discussed in chapter 3, the districts of black legislators have many things in common: their constituents typically are low-income, possess low levels of education, and are predominantly black. This is typical of the vast majority of districts represented by black-caucus members across the country, not just in Louisiana.[14] Consequently, the types of bills introduced are the product not only of a legislator's race but also of the type of area he or she represents. In other words, legislators' policy agendas reflect the specific needs of their communities and suggest a correlation between race and geography.

From a representational standpoint, it is often difficult to discern whether race or constituency drives black legislative behavior, since most black legislators represent majority-minority districts. However, there is quite a range within these districts, from one having barely a black majority (53.1% black) to one that is more than 90 percent black. Given this spectrum, we examine the impact of district characteristics on the agenda of LLBC members along with other important demographic factors, including the percentage of the district population on welfare, the percentage with a college degree, and the median district income.

As previous findings argue, many black-interest issues have to do with poverty and the lack of opportunities for minorities. Therefore, we may expect LLBC members representing poorer and less-educated constituencies to focus more on black-interest legislation, while we may expect those representing districts with more black constituents to focus more on race-specific issues.

In addition to constituency, an individual member's personal characteristics may influence the agenda he or she sets. Using the personal dimensions discussed in chapter 3, we incorporate the results of our survey to test for agenda differences between LLBC members. Specifically, we examine self-reported ideology, educational attainment, and income. Unfortunately, we cannot simply replicate our multivariate analysis from models 1 and 2 in table 4.2 due to the small sample size when focusing only on the LLBC.[15] Instead, we compare various district and personal characteristics to discover patterns in agenda setting. In order to test these hypotheses, we convert our count bill-introduction variables into percentages based on the total number of bills a legislator introduced in a session. This helps control for the overall activity level of the member. In this analysis, we exclude the two special sessions because of the small number of bills introduced in those sessions by most members.

We find quite a large variation among LLBC members in terms of the percentage of their agendas devoted to black-interest issues. For black-interest legislation, the mean is 20.69, with a standard deviation of 14.65 and a range of 0 percent to 59.62 percent. For race-specific legislation, the mean is 2.70, with a standard deviation of 5.01 and a range of 0 percent to 26.67 percent. Overall, black-interest legislation made up a sizable portion of LLBC members' agendas but in most cases did not constitute a majority. On the other hand, race-specific legislation made up a very small portion of most black members' agendas.

To determine whether there were any district-level influences on the agendas, we examine correlation coefficients for each district-level variable for all legislation and for bills only (table 4.4). These correlations give us an opportunity to look for any bivariate patterns absent the statistical power to present more detailed regression analyses.

Starting with all legislation, we find that members from poorer districts dedicated a greater percentage of their agendas to both black-interest and race-specific issues. There is a moderate correlation between a member's median district income and the percentage of black-interest (-.28) and race-specific (-.31) bills introduced. The negative relationship

TABLE 4.4. Correlation between District Characteristics and Black-Interest and Race-Specific Agendas, 2005 and 2006 Regular Sessions

District Characteristic	% Black-Interest	% Race-Specific
All Legislation		
% black	-.07	.23
Median income	-.28*	-.31*
% college degree	.07	.04
% households on welfare	.31*	.39**
N	62	62
Bills Only		
% black	-.11	.24
Median income	-.21	.36**
% college degree	.01	.05
% households on welfare	.15	.41**
N	62	62

Note: Each cell contains the Pearson's correlation coefficient.

$*p < .05, **p < .01, ***p < .001$

illustrates, for example, that as a district's median income increases, the percentage of bills focused on black-interest legislation decreases. For a more specific measure of district poverty, we include the percentage of households receiving welfare and find a slightly stronger relationship, especially for race-specific legislation (.39). These findings are not surprising in terms of general black-interest legislation, since many of the policy areas deal with issues relating to poverty and social welfare. As a result, members responded by introducing bills involving black interests. For the race-specific legislation, we do not find a significant relationship for the percentage of black constituents in the district as expected, but rather the same income and poverty characteristics. This suggests that members are not more likely to introduce race-specific legislation simply based on the racial composition of their districts; rather the link between issues of poverty and race remains.

We conduct the same analysis for substantive bills only. This allows us to see whether there are any differences between the members' agendas that included symbolic resolutions and their substantive focus in the legislature. Here we find slightly surprising results. The income and poverty measures are no longer significant on the general black-interest measure, suggesting that part of members' black-interest policy agendas may indeed be symbolic in nature. In fact, we do not see any significant correlations between the percentage of substantive black-interest legislation a member introduces and the member's district characteristics. For race-specific legislation, we find the same results as in the top half of table 4.4: members from districts with higher median incomes and lower welfare rates introduced less legislation specifically dealing with race. Overall, these findings suggest that race is not the only factor influencing how LLBC members represent their constituents; the economics of their districts also appear to influence members' agendas.

Next, we examine the impact of individual characteristics on members' decision making. From our surveys, we measure the level of education, income, and ideological self-placement of our respondents, as these are among the primary factors determining political differences among both elites and the mass public. According to conventional views about the influence of these factors, we expect liberal members to focus more of their agendas on black-interest and race-specific issues, and we expect those with higher incomes to devote less of their agendas to these issues. For level of education, we do not have a clear expectation. On one hand, we might expect that as members attain graduate and professional degrees, they become more aware of the problems and inequities facing the black community and may devote more of their agendas to these issues. On the other hand, however, perhaps higher levels of education correlate with higher income and less liberal ideologies, which may lead to a decreased focus on issues specifically related to the black community.

Table 4.5 shows the mean differences between demographic characteristics, along with the t-statistic. We find little evidence that individual characteristics significantly influence members' agendas. It does not appear that either ideology or income has a significant impact on all legislation or on substantive bills only. This may be in part because of our small sample and because of personal similarities (especially in income) between our

TABLE 4.5. Personal Characteristics and Black-Interest and Race-Specific Agendas, 2005 and 2006 Regular Sessions

Personal Characteristic	Black-Interest % (N)	t	Race-Specific % (N)	t
All Legislation				
Education				
Bachelor's degree or less	14.21 (17)		0.53 (17)	
Advanced degree	24.05 (28)	-2.27*	3.04 (28)	-2.28*
Ideological self-placement				
Liberal	21.51 (20)		2.07 (20)	
Moderate/conservative	19.39 (25)	-.47	2.12 (25)	.04
Income				
Over $70,000	18.84 (38)		1.76 (38)	
$70,000 or less	28.46 (7)	1.61	3.91 (7)	1.41
Bills Only				
Education				
Bachelor's degree or less	17.24 (17)		0 (17)	
Advanced degree	26.66 (28)	-1.93	2.50 (28)	-2.41*
Ideological self-placement				
Liberal	22.65 (20)		1.58 (20)	
Moderate/conservative	23.47 (25)	.16	1.53 (25)	-.04
Income				
Over $70,000	21.16 (38)		1.38 (38)	
$70,000 or less	33.62 (7)	1.90	2.48 (7)	.75

Note: One representative joined between the 2005 and 2006 sessions, making for a total sample of 45. Each cell represents the percentage of each group's introductions by area; group size is given in parentheses. The t-test statistic tests for significant differences between groups.

*$p < .05$, **$p < .01$, ***$p < .001$

respondents. However, we argue that this result reflects similar ideas about the importance of representing the black community and black interests among all black legislators, whether liberal or moderate and regardless of income bracket. We do find significant differences based on level of education. Members with advanced degrees (professional or graduate) introduced more general black-interest and race-specific legislation. Three of the four t-tests show a statistically significant difference, with the fourth barely outside conventional levels of significance. These findings suggest that with more education comes more attention to the black community or the issues most closely associated with the black community.

We are not suggesting that the bivariate test results in tables 4.4 and 4.5 provide a definitive picture of how district and individual characteristics influence black members' agendas. However, these findings are suggestive and provide more details than many studies on the topic have provided. Overall, it appears that members do respond to the needs of their districts, as LLBC members from poorer districts spend more time on race-specific legislation of both a substantive and a symbolic nature. For more general black-interest legislation, members appear to focus more on symbolic resolutions than on purely substantive bills. We do not find any correlation between either the individual member's ideology or his or her personal income and the likelihood of focusing his or her agenda on more black-interest issues. However, members with higher levels of education tend to introduce more legislation dealing with both black-interest and race-specific topics.

Cosponsorship

In both the surveys and the interviews, several members indicated that caucus membership contributed to unity and working together. "You have such a small group," one member pointed out, "and if we don't unite and work together, and support one another, then we won't be able to accomplish our goals." Extending this idea to LLBC members' joining together in order to pass legislation as a group, we examined the rates of bill cosponsorship among them. Bill cosponsorship is a low-cost strategy employed by legislators when building coalitions and expressing support for legislation.[16] If members of the LLBC believe that working together is a key to legislative success, then we should observe higher rates of cosponsorship among LLBC members than among other groups in the legislature.

Table 4.6 shows determinants of cosponsorship for all legislation except concurrent resolutions across the four sessions. Our dependent variable is the number of LLBC cosponsors when a piece of legislation was first introduced in the original chamber. We give the number of cosponsors at this point in the process since we believe that it sends the strongest signal of initial support.[17] This count variable fits with the other models used in this chapter, and due to overdispersion in the data, we use a negative-binomial model. Our primary independent variable of interest is group membership for the bill sponsor, and we control for most of the same factors found in table 4.2. If the LLBC uses a strategy of group unity, then we would expect to find more LLBC cosponsors of legislation introduced by other caucus members.

Overall, legislation averaged just over three cosponsors, with 73 percent of all bills initially having no cosponsors, and the average number of LLBC cosponsors was just under one, with 88 percent of legislation having no black cosponsors. In table 4.6 we find no evidence suggesting that LLBC members are more likely to cosponsor other caucus members' legislation, since the LLBC group variable does not reach statistical significance. Our findings indicate that senate LLBC members are less likely to cosponsor bills than their house counterparts. Furthermore, black members are more likely to cosponsor substantive rather than symbolic bills, and they are more likely to cosponsor legislation when the total number of cosponsors is large.

We also examined the cosponsorship rates among the groups and found no substantive differences in terms of the actual percentages based on who introduced the legislation or the type of legislation. This analysis also confirmed the findings in table 4.6 that LLBC members are not any more likely to cosponsor bills introduced by other LLBC members than any other legislation. These findings do not match the rhetoric from our interviews, especially with LLBC members in the state senate. This is an interesting discrepancy given the importance several of our interviewees placed on working with other LLBC members. Perhaps we looked at the wrong point in the legislative process for strategic cosponsorship; maybe the members of the Louisiana legislature have other informal means of communicating support and preferences to one another.

TABLE 4.6. Influences on Bill Cosponsorship

Variable	Number of LLBC Cosponsors[a]
LLBC membership[b]	1938 (.1984)
Republican Party membership[b]	.2036 (.2033)
Orleans Caucus membership	.1952 (.2492)
Gender	-.2584 (.1732)
Seniority	-.002 (.0110)
Party leadership	.1573 (.2456)
Committee leadership	.2833 (.1826)
Chamber	-.4747 (.1892)*
Type of legislation	2.386 (1.066)*
Number of cosponsors	.1505 (.0223)***
Black-interest legislation	.1242 (.1984)
Race-specific legislation	.6907 (.6797)
2005 special session[c]	.6499 (.3487)
2006 special session[c]	1.107 (.3045)***
2006 regular session[c]	-.8213 (.1709)***
Constant	-3.92 (1.073)***
α	8.696 (.9418)
N	5,503
Log pseudo-likelihood	-2734.58

Note: Dependent variable = count of LLBC cosponsors on an introduced bill. Models are clustered by member. Each cell contains the coefficient estimate, with robust standard error in parentheses.

[a] Negative binomial regression, robust standard errors in parentheses.
[b] White Democrats are the base category.
[c] The 2005 regular session is the base category.

$*p < .05, **p < .01, ***p < .001$

Conclusion

Our initial analysis of agenda setting by black legislators confirms the findings of previous studies and adds to the literature showing that minority legislators are more likely to set an agenda that deals with issues related to their own minority group. This is not a new finding, but is one we should keep in mind in the next two chapters. Additionally, it is important to show that the Louisiana legislature is not unique in how its members set their agendas.

Our findings show that black legislators are much more likely to introduce legislation that deals with both general black-interest policy issues and more race-specific issues related to the black community. One argument is that minority legislators can be more successful on symbolic issues and may introduce more resolutions to represent their constituents on these matters. In general, we did not find any evidence to support this thesis, because, as our results indicate, on several occasions LLBC members focused more on a substantive than on a symbolic agenda.

While our analysis goes beyond most studies on agenda setting by examining issues specific to the black legislators in the state, it is important to note that our findings suggest that both district- and individual-level factors influence black legislators and the agendas they set. On the district level, legislators from poorer districts spent more of their agenda on issues related to the black community. This was the one place that we found suggestive evidence for the symbolic-representation thesis, since there was a more significant correlation between poorer districts and a general black-interest agenda in the "all legislation" test than in the test examining just bills.

Overall, legislators respond to the needs of their constituents. As history shows, many black constituents are concerned about issues of poverty because they are living in it, and as a result, black legislators adopt these issues. They become wrapped up in the black community and their needs. While all members represented majority-minority districts, our findings do not suggest that members representing more homogenous districts were more likely to focus on black-interest issues. On the individual level, more than ideology or income, having earned an advanced degree appeared to drive members to focus their agendas on black-interest issues.

Finally, members stressed the unity of the caucus and the fact that they must support each other in order to have success in the legislature. However, we do not find any evidence of this at the agenda-setting stage. This is not so surprising, since the beginning part of the process allows individual members to announce their own agendas to reflect their personal policy goals and district policy needs. LLBC members may not see a need to use their political capital this early in the process or to attach their support to bills ultimately doomed to fail.

We have shown that black members are more likely to introduce bills relating to the black community and that certain district- and individual-level factors account for some of the variation in the portion of their agendas that LLBC members devote to these issues. In the next two chapters, we look at what happens to these agendas and examine whether black members are able to translate their agendas into policy success.

5

Turning Black-Interest Agendas into Policy

In February 2006, during the special legislative session devoted to hurricane recovery, the Louisiana Legislative Black Caucus faced a bitter defeat in the house when it attempted to pass legislation to place satellite voting locations around the state for New Orleans evacuees to use in that year's city elections. Upon the final roll-call tally of 46 ayes, 53 nays, and 5 abstentions, the 23 members of the LLBC walked out of the chamber to show their dissatisfaction with the outcome and to charge "blatant racism" on the part of those who had voted against them.[1] A few months later, during the regular session, with much less media attention, the LLBC once again faced losing a roll-call vote on a bill central to the caucus's agenda, this time in the senate. The LLBC was attempting to garner support for a bill to reduce life sentences for felons convicted on heroin charges. This bill was one of 54 they publicly placed on their agenda for the regular session. The measure failed by two votes upon its third reading.

Are these losing votes the norm for the LLBC? In this chapter, we examine what happens to legislation after it enters the legislative arena. In chapter 4 we saw that LLBC members introduced legislation that focused on the same general policy areas as did legislation introduced by white members of the Louisiana legislature, yet members of the LLBC were more likely to introduce legislation related to black interests. In this chapter, we move from the agenda-setting stage to the legislative stage to examine possible differences between what happens to the bills introduced by members of the LLBC and what happens to those introduced by white Democrats and by Republicans.

The caucus plays a particularly important role during the legislative stage. Some LLBC members felt that the Black Caucus served primarily to get support for members' policies. One LLBC member stated, "The Black Caucus supports me in legislation. Sometimes I feel that if it hadn't been for the Caucus, I would not have gotten a bill out of committee. We support one another in getting legislation passed." LLBC members made it very clear that they sought the support of the caucus because it was a large bloc and because quite often their bills would not have made it out of committee or passed in the legislature without its support. Here we explore the latter part of the previous statement by looking at bill outcomes from several different perspectives.

Factors Influencing Legislative Success

Ultimately, bill passage is the fundamental job of any legislature and one of its jobs that is most visible to the public. Given this importance, scholars have focused on identifying factors that lead to greater legislative success. Mark C. Ellickson identified three main categories of factors associated with influencing legislative success: institutional, personal, and environmental.[2] For institutional factors, the role of party is crucial. Being a member of the majority party is always an important component of overall legislative success.[3] A recent study suggests that along with being in the majority party, being a loyal party member increases legislative success.[4] Another common finding is that seniority increases legislative success.[5] Both previous research and conventional wisdom link several other institutional factors to legislative success. Being on the committee that receives a bill is related to an increase in legislative success, as the individual member has a more direct role in working the bill through the process.[6] Additionally, being in a position of either party or committee leadership is also important, as leaders tend to have sway over rank-and-file members at voting time.[7]

Any discussion of the legislative process cannot overlook the overarching assumption of most research on legislative behavior and representation, namely, that reelection is a legislator's primary goal.[8] The goal of reelection is often intertwined with the goal of making good public policy, at least in the eyes of one's constituents. As a result, it is important to consider a member's electoral or environmental situation when examining his or her legislative success. Previous findings generally suggest that electorally safe members have more legislative success for a variety of reasons, including more flexibility to pursue a successful agenda and work with other members on compromises that often lead to success.[9]

This is not to suggest that institutional and environmental factors drive all legislative success. Without a doubt, personal political acumen is also an important factor. Some legislators are more successful because they act more strategically and play the game better than others.[10] One way that researchers have measured this ability has been to look at a legislator's activity levels; they generally found that "selectively active legislators are able to overcome institutional impediments and see their legislative agendas to fruition."[11]

Membership in a minority group can be a significant impediment to legislative success. Lani Guinier's book *The Tyranny of the Majority,* which was at the center of her controversial and ultimately doomed nomination as U.S. assistant attorney general for civil rights, calls attention to this fact.[12] In the book, she argues that blacks especially face an uphill struggle to win policy battles in Congress. In her view, attaining office is not sufficient to influence policy, due to the likelihood of racially based voting coalitions and the perpetual minority status of black legislators.

One factor that may lead to failed policy outcomes is not necessarily outright racial prejudice but the use of voting cues. Because of a lack of time and a large workload, legislators often use voting cues. One important cue is what they know about a bill's sponsors and its supporters or opposition.[13] White legislators may have built up a heuristic or cue that tells them a black-sponsored bill is simply too liberal for them to support or too out of context to benefit their constituency. The one exception to this may be a bill that deals specifically with a black interest area: white legislators may see LLBC members as experts in the policy area and shift their voting cues accordingly, which allows black members a greater likelihood of success.[14]

We shall now look at previous studies examining minority legislators' success in passing bills. These studies have generally found that minority legislators are less likely to pass legislation than their white and male counterparts. In terms of gender, most previous research indicates that bills introduced by women are less likely to become law than those introduced by men.[15] However, more recent research finds that bills introduced by women are just as likely to become law as those introduced by men.[16] A few studies have examined the success of Latino legislators, mostly at the state level, and found that while they too are less successful than white legislators in getting bills passed, they have gained the power to block legislation in certain states.[17]

In terms of black legislators, the same trend generally holds true. Kathleen Bratton and Kerry Haynie found that blacks in three states were significantly less likely to get legislation passed than whites.[18] In several studies on the Mississippi house, Byron Orey found that black legislators were much less successful than their white colleagues, while Orey and his colleagues found similar results for black male legislators but no significant difference in bill-passage success between black female and white male legislators.[19] Other studies paint similar overall pictures of minorities as less successful in the legislative process, but some studies find positive results in very specific situations.[20]

Analysis
Overview of Bill Passage

We begin our analysis by looking at the similarities and differences between LLBC members, white Democrats, and Republicans in terms of bill passage by policy area. Table 5.1 highlights similar patterns in areas of passed legislation. Policies in the areas of revenue, taxation, and appropriations; state government; and law and crime made the top three of each group. Completing the top five for the LLBC were education and insurance policies; for white Democrats, transportation and banking, finance, and commerce; and for Republicans, health care and transportation. While the groups passed legislation in very similar areas, no group had a dominant hold on any policy area, as the top policies for each group made up 20 percent or less of the total legislation passed by the groups' members. Finally, turning back to the top agenda items discussed in the previous chapter, we find a consistency between the top policy areas for bill introductions and those for bill passage. Overall, this consistency indicates that all three groups are most successful in passing bills within the areas on which they focus their agendas. Table 5.1 does not indicate any policy bias in terms of what issues members put on their agendas and the policies they are able to turn into law.

TABLE 5.1. Legislation Passage Rates for Groups' Top Five Policy Areas

Policy Area	LLBC Rank	LLBC % Passed	White Democrats Rank	White Democrats % Passed	Republicans Rank	Republicans % Passed
Appropriations	4	9.25	1	17.58	3	9.56
Education	5	7.88	—		—	
Finance and Commerce	—		4	8.07	—	
Health	—		—		4	7.57
Insurance	3	9.59	—		—	
Law and Crime	2	14.73	3	12.39	1	20.52
State Government	1	17.12	2	14.41	2	14.14
Transportation	—		5	6.77	4	7.57

Note: Based on bills only.

While we know that members of the LLBC passed legislation in similar policy areas to those of white Democrats and Republicans, we do not know their rate of success. Table 5.2 shows the overall passage rates for the three groups using means-comparison tests. We determined the rate by dividing the number of bills that became law by the total number of bills introduced by each group. We find LLBC members to have the lowest passage rates. Looking at all introduced legislation, LLBC members passed 52.59 percent of their bills into law, compared with 58.37 percent for white Democrats and 56.35 percent for Republicans, a statistically significant difference in both cases. This shows that black members, who were also all Democrats and members of the majority, had lower success rates than the minority Republicans.

We know that bills focus on substantive issues, and resolutions tend to be more symbolic in nature. Symbolic representation is one area in which black members may have more success; if this holds true for the LLBC, then we should find higher passage rates for resolutions. Once again, we find the LLBC to have the lowest passage rates for both bills and resolutions. Looking first at bills only, members of the LLBC passed 31.81 percent of the bills they introduced, compared with 44.66 percent for white Demo-

TABLE 5.2. Legislation Passage Rates by Group and Type of Legislation

Group	Bills % (No.)	t	Resolutions % (No.)	t	Bills and Resolutions % (No.)	t
All Legislation						
LLBC	31.81 (918)	—	88.66 (529)	—	52.59 (1,447)	—
White Democrats	44.66 (1,554)	-6.35***	91.22 (649)	-1.46	58.37 (2,203)	3.45***
Republicans	39.37 (1,275)	3.65***	92.63 (597)	-2.30*	56.35 (1,872)	-2.16*
		2.84^^		-0.91		1.30
Black-Interest Legislation						
LLBC	30.87 (230)	—	84.42 (77)	—	44.30 (307)	—
White Democrats	45.31 (245)	-3.26**	83.93 (56)	0.08	52.49 (301)	2.02*
Republicans	41.86 (215)	-2.42*	82.05 (39)	0.32	48.03 (254)	0.88
		0.74		0.24		1.04
Non-Black-Interest Legislation						
LLBC	32.12 (688)	—	89.38 (452)	—	54.82 (1,140)	—
White Democrats	45.54 (1,309)	-5.41***	91.91 (593)	-1.40	59.31 (1,902)	-2.42*
Republicans	38.87 (1,060)	-2.87**	93.37 (558)	2.27*	57.66 (1,618)	-1.48
		2.78^^		-0.95		0.96

Note: The t-score is the independent sample t-test statistic.

Significance difference between LLBC and White Democrats/Republicans: *p < .05, **p < .01, ***p < .001.
Significance difference between White Democrats and Republicans: ^p < .05, ^^p < .01, ^^^p < .001.

crats and 39.37 percent for Republicans, and once again both differences are statistically significant. We find that the majority white Democrats had significantly more success on substantive bills than LLBC members and Republicans, but the Republicans, who were in the minority, were more successful than the majority-party LLBC members. Turning to symbolic issues, we find that all three groups passed more than 85 percent of the resolutions they introduced. This is not surprising given that most resolutions are noncontroversial and that many members use them as a tool for constituent service. However, the Republicans actually surpassed the other two groups in the percentage of their own resolutions passed, a statistically significant difference from the LLBC. Overall, the majority white Democrats had no need to block the passage of these symbolic gestures, which had no bearing on substantive public policy.

Next, we break down passage rates for black-interest legislation and find a similar pattern. For all black-interest legislation, LLBC members were once again the least successful in passing legislation, at 44.30 percent, while white Democrats were the most successful, at 52.49 percent, which represents a significant difference. While the Republicans were slightly more successful than the LLBC, the difference is not significant. Yet, when we look at black-interest bills only, the significant difference reemerges, as the LLBC success rate dropped to 30.87 percent, compared with 45.31 percent for the white Democrats and 41.86 percent for the Republicans. While the difference is not statistically significant, LLBC members did have more success passing black-interest resolutions than the other groups, even though for all groups black-interest resolutions had the lowest passage rates of any type of resolutions. This shows that black members are no less successful in passing symbolic gestures to represent their constituents. It also shows that even in areas of particular concern to the black community, the LLBC is less successful than either the white Democrats or the Republicans.

For non-black-interest legislation, the gap is smaller between the success of the LLBC and the success of the white Democrats, but the LLBC members are still significantly less likely to pass legislation. However, legislation introduced by the LLBC is most likely to pass if it is non-black-interest legislation (54.82% for all legislation), but this percentage is mainly driven by the higher passage rates of resolutions and not substantive bills, as the likelihood of passing a substantive bill is only slightly higher for non-black-interest legislation than for black-interest legislation (32.12% versus 30.87%).

From table 5.2, it appears that LLBC members faced an uphill battle to successfully implement their agenda even though they were part of the controlling majority, since they generally had less success than Republicans. However, these findings are merely suggestive. In order to further probe this question, we model how far a bill goes in the legislative process.

The Likelihood of Passing Legislation

As table 5.2 shows, members of the LLBC had the lowest passage rates in almost all situations, even though they were part of the majority party. What factors drive these results? Since we are interested in the entire legislative process, we account for the different steps in the legislative process to discover whether LLBC members have more or less success than other members at different stages in the process. The Louisiana legislature, like all other legislative bodies, tends to kill more legislation than it passes, as there are many more ways for legislation to die than for it to become law. For example, a bill might never make it out of committee; it might fail to come up for a vote on the floor; it might fail a floor vote; it might be stopped in the other chamber; it might not survive a conference committee or a gubernatorial veto. These possibilities can be grouped into three key categories that capture the most important components of legislative bill making: (1) bills that died in committee in the originating chamber; (2) bills that died on the floor of the originating chamber, somewhere in the other chamber, or in conference committee; and (3) bills that became law.[21] We thus have three distinct categories that capture aspects of the process beyond a simple dichotomous measure of whether or not a bill became law. These categories also provide more detail about the LLBC's effectiveness in navigating the legislative process.

Looking at these categories, we find that 43 percent of all legislation died in committee, while 40 percent became law and the remaining 17 percent died somewhere on the floor of the originating chamber or in the other chamber. Based on the categories described above, we use an ordinal logit model to analyze legislative success. We use this model since the categories represent how far in the legislative process a bill made it, from not going anywhere (dying in committee) to becoming law.[22] Using independent variables similar to those used in chapter 4, we are interested in how successful LLBC members are in relation to white Democrats and Republicans in passing legislation, controlling for other important factors.

Our real concern in these models is the institutional characteristics of the legislature, most notably the group identification of the legislators. We expect members of the LLBC to be less successful in navigating the legislative process than their white Democratic counterparts. Given the distinctive districts they represent and the history of marginalization of minority legislators, we have no reason to expect the white majority to see the LLBC as equal legislating partners when it comes to passing legislation. Potentially more interesting is the success of the LLBC compared with the minority Republicans. If the Democrats were unified in the legislature, then the LLBC should have been more successful than its GOP counterparts. However, as discussed in chapter 3, if the white Democrats were more focused on constituent similarities and not partisan labels, then the Republicans might be more successful than the LLBC, since most white Democratic districts had more in common with Republican districts than with LLBC members' districts. Additionally, we consider whether a member is part of the Orleans Caucus. Given the divide in the state between New Orleans and the rest of the state, and given the distinctiveness of representing New Orleans, members of the Orleans Caucus might be at a disadvantage when it comes to passing legislation. We also look at the gender of the legislator, since women make up another important minority group within the legislature and previous research shows that women tend to have a different legislative agenda, with a different success rate, than their male counterparts.[23]

We also control for other institutional characteristics. We consider seniority, being a part of the leadership, and being a committee member as potentially significant in working through the legislative process. The longer a legislator has been in office, the more likely he or she is to understand how to work the process and compromise and bargain with other members.[24] Being a part of the (chamber or committee) leadership has many benefits, and legislators who belong to the leadership are generally more effective than other members.[25] In addition, being a member of the committee in which a bill is referred should help a legislator get that bill out

Turning Black-Interest Agendas into Policy

of committee, if not help get it passed, since he or she should be in a better position to work on the bill throughout the process. Finally, we control for chamber, in order to test for any differences between the house and the senate, and for the legislative session.

We also consider other factors that might influence the success of passing legislation.[26] In terms of the environment, we look at district competitiveness and district partisanship. With respect to district competitiveness, one argument is that legislators from competitive districts are less likely to assert a leadership role due to the time they spend worrying about the competition in their home districts and attempting to secure support there. Thus, their focus may shift to constituent service and away from the policy arena.[27] A counterargument is that legislators from competitive districts feel more pressured to secure favorable public policy for their constituents and will spend more time gathering support than legislators from safe districts, who may have more leeway to shirk their duties. Since electoral vulnerability is not central to our theoretical argument, we simply note the competing possibilities and control for district competitiveness in our models with the percentage of the vote a legislator received in his or her previous election.[28]

We also control for district partisanship using registration data.[29] Louisiana updates its voter-registration rolls every quarter, and we use the registration figures from closest to the start of each of the four legislative sessions. This allows us to track the modest changes between the sessions. Here we consider the percentage of registered Democrats in a district, as legislators, regardless of group identification, who represent districts with a large number of Democrats or Republicans may have different incentives to work with legislators beyond their group when navigating the legislative process. We expect legislators who represent more Democrats to be more successful, since they are more likely to introduce and work for bills that the majority of Democrats agree with. To account for personal factors, we look at the activity levels of legislators, thinking that legislators who introduce more bills may be more successful than less active legislators. We include the total number of bills a legislator introduced in each session.

We examine legislation-specific factors, since some types of legislation may be more likely to pass or die in committee regardless of who introduced them. We look at whether a bill deals with a black-interest policy,

TABLE 5.3. Estimates of Bill Passage

Variable	Model 1: All Legislation	Model 2: Bills Only
LLBC membership[a]	-.418 (.1224)***	-.472 (.1285)***
Republican Party membership[a]	.1865 (.1526)	.1861 (.1639)
Orleans Caucus membership	-.321 (.1471)*	-.348 (.1553)*
Years in office	.0025 (.0054)	.0041 (.0051)
Chamber	-.220 (.0969)*	-.235 (.1031)*
Gender	-.348 (.1328)**	-.307 (.1345)*
Party leadership	.0264 (.1414)	.1233 (.2341)
Committee leadership	.4560 (.1207)***	.4424 (.1207)***
Committee membership	.5498 (.0907)***	.5301 (.0946)***
% vote in last election	.0029 (.0023)	.0031 (.0023)
% Registered Democrats	.0165 (.0065)*	.0183 (.0070)**
Black-interest policy	.1724 (.0912)	.1541 (.0959)
Type of legislation	-1.07 (.2182)***	
Number of cosponsors	.0447 (.0073)***	.0436 (.0070)***
Substitute bill	1.388 (.2166)***	1.410 (.2221)***
Total introductions	-.002 (.0044)	-.003 (.0044)
2005 special session[b]	-.891 (.1647)***	-.893 (.1629)***
2006 special session[b]	-.628 (.2050)**	-.509 (.2090)*
2006 regular session[b]	-.127 (.0898)	-.091 (.0958)
Cut 1	-.409 (.5624)	.8054 (.5160)
Cut 2	.3457 (.5572)	1.579 (.5087)
Log pseudo-likelihood	-4206.50	-3922.90
Pseudo R^2	0.06	0.05
N	4,320	3,985

Note: Ordered logit estimation is clustered by legislator. The dependent variables are coded as follows: 0 = died in committee, 1 = died on floor or in other chamber or was vetoed, 2 = became law. Each cell contains the coefficient estimate, with robust standard error in parentheses.

[a] White Democrats are the base category.
[b] The 2005 regular session is the base category.

*$p < .05$, **$p < .01$, ***$p < .001$

whether it is a substantive bill or a resolution, and the number of cosponsors it had when it was first introduced. As discussed in detail in chapter 4, black-interest legislation may not be a focus or concern of legislators outside the LLBC and may receive less attention in the legislative process. If this is true, then we would expect black-interest policies to be more likely to die in committee and less likely to become law. Given the importance of substantive bills compared with resolutions, we expect bills to be less likely to pass than resolutions.[30]

Resolutions afford an easy, usually noncontroversial way for members to symbolically represent their members or address issues of concern. Since they are not binding and make no substantive policy changes, an easy way for the majority white Democrats to pacify the LLBC would be to refrain from blocking passage of resolutions while obstructing LLBC attempts to pass substantive bills on policies that are outside the agenda of the rest of the Democratic majority, as suggested by table 5.2 above. We also test a model that looks only at bills in order to focus specifically on substantive legislation. Additionally, we expect the number of cosponsors to influence the likelihood of passage. The more support a bill has from the beginning, the more likely it will be to pass out of committee and become law. Cosponsorship is an easy and cheap signal of support. Finally, we control for whether a bill was a substitute or not. Substitute bills replace entire pieces of legislation, generally toward the end of the process (although some are introduced in committee), and may have an easier time of becoming law because of the point at which they enter the process.

Table 5.3 reports the estimates from the two models on bill passage. A quick glance at the coefficients suggests that LLBC members are less likely than white Democrats (the reference group) to have legislation move toward becoming law, while there is no significant difference between Republicans' and white Democrats' likely success. Additionally, we find a negative influence for the Orleans Caucus. Interestingly, we do not find a significant relationship between black-interest bills and bill outcomes. The rest of our control variables generally behave in the expected manner, with the exception of gender, as women appear to be more successful than men in the legislative process. Since logit coefficients do not lend themselves to straightforward interpretation, we present predicted probabilities for a more specific discussion on the relationships between the variables.

Figures 5.1 and 5.2 illustrate the likelihood of a bill's passing through the various stages of the legislative process using our key variables of interest. In each case, the remaining variables are held at their appropriate means or modal categories to represent the average legislator. This process allows us to predict a bill's outcome based on the characteristics that vary among legislators. Figure 5.1 shows probabilities varied by group and policy area for model 2, bills only. In every situation we find LLBC members' legislation to be the most likely to be stopped in a committee and the least likely to become law. This confirms the findings in table 5.2, even when controlling for other important factors.

Another interesting finding that emerges from figure 5.1 is that when all other factors are held constant, Republicans were more likely than white Democrats to pass a bill. This seems counterintuitive, since the Republicans were in the minority in both chambers. Overall, as table 5.2 shows, the white Democrats were more successful in passing legislation, but when controlling for institutional, environmental, and policy factors, the model actually predicts Republicans to be slightly more successful. However, this is not a statistically significant relationship. Finally, figure 5.1 shows that black-interest legislation was actually more likely to pass than non-black-interest legislation, regardless of the sponsor. However, once again, according to the model, this is not a statistically significant difference. LLBC-sponsored black-interest legislation was about 3.5 percent more

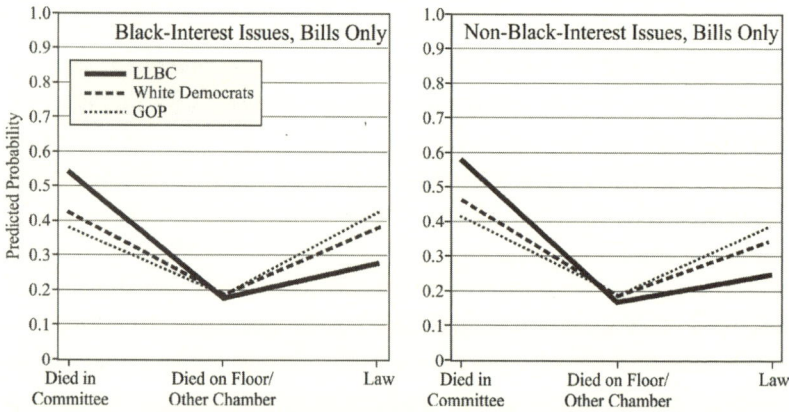

FIGURE 5.1. Predicted Probabilities for Bill Passage by Group

Turning Black-Interest Agendas into Policy

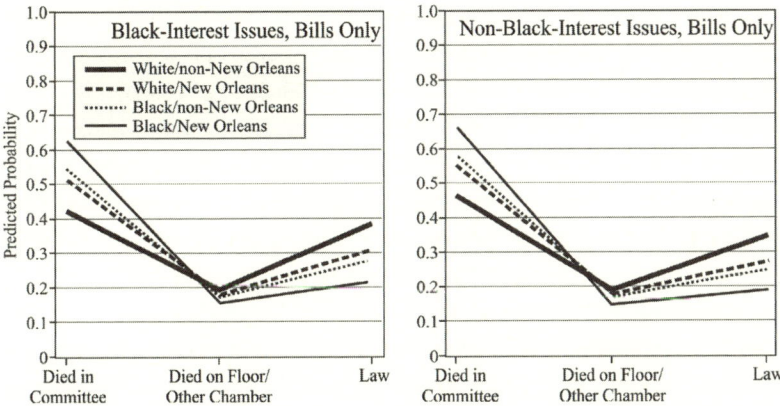

FIGURE 5.2. Predicted Probabilities for Bill Passage by LLBC and New Orleans Delegations

likely to pass than non-black-interest legislation, which suggests that the LLBC was more successful in steering bills of particular importance to the black community toward passage. We see a similar pattern for legislation sponsored by both white Democrats and Republicans: when non-black legislators sponsored black-interest legislation, it was actually more likely to pass.

Several possible scenarios may explain this outcome. First, if the legislation resulted in a positive policy change for black constituents, then the LLBC was most likely to support the bill regardless of the sponsor. This would give a bill more support and increase its likelihood of passage. Second, if a bill dealt with an area of concern to the black community but proposed a negative policy shift for the community, then the LLBC was not likely to support the bill. However, as we shall see in the next chapter, the LLBC did not have the numbers to kill legislation in a floor vote when both white Democrats and Republicans united behind a bill. According to the first scenario, this would mean that the LLBC was having a positive effect throughout the legislature by spreading the issues and concerns of the black community beyond its members. However, according to the second scenario, this would mean that the LLBC and its message were being marginalized by white members from both parties.

Another important finding is that legislators representing New Orleans were also at a disadvantage in the Louisiana legislative process. Figure 5.2

shows the predicted probabilities for bill outcomes for LLBC members and for the Orleans delegation. The figure focuses on substantive bills only from model 2. Here we find clear and distinct disadvantages for black members who represented New Orleans. For both types of policies, they were 6 percent less likely to have a bill become law than the next lowest group (non–New Orleans LLBC members) and more than 15 percent less likely than the highest group (non–New Orleans whites). While white legislators representing New Orleans were more successful than their LLBC counterparts both outside and inside New Orleans, they were still much less successful than white legislators from the rest of the state (roughly 8% for both policy types). Additionally, New Orleans whites were only slightly more successful (about 1.5%–2.0%) than black legislators from outside New Orleans.

Overall, figure 5.2 shows that race is not the only cleavage in Louisiana politics. The divide between New Orleans and the rest of the state is a common theme in Louisiana politics, as it is in other states with major metropolitan areas. However, a black legislator from New Orleans is the least likely to successfully represent his or her constituents, regardless of the type of policy, by passing new legislation. LLBC members from outside New Orleans have the second lowest rates of policy passage, but white members from New Orleans have similar probabilities that put them in a distinctly lower category than white members from outside the Orleans Caucus. It appears that white legislators from outside New Orleans have the clearest path to policy success, given their larger numbers in the legislature, and the white members from New Orleans have more in common with their LLBC counterparts, at least in terms of expected bill outcomes.

Committee Outcomes

Across the board, black legislators were less likely to pass legislation than both white Democrats and, surprisingly, Republicans. The predicted probabilities show this holding true in every situation. Conversely, members of the LLBC had the highest rate of bills dying in committee. As our analysis shows, it was in committee, and not on the chamber floor, that LLBC members struggled. The three groups had a fairly low (14%–19%), almost equal chance of having a piece of legislation stall on the floor. Given this finding, we take a closer look at the committee stage to examine why black legislators struggle at this point in the process.

In many ways, this first stage is the most important, because once legislation leaves a committee, it will most likely pass in a unanimous or nearly unanimous floor vote in both chambers. Committees serve as the gatekeepers of the legislative process. It is in committees that most of the debating and amending is done. Committees can stop legislation before all the members of the legislature have an opportunity to consider it. At this important stage, what factors influence the ability of LLBC-sponsored legislation to make it out of committee? We examine this question using OLS regression with robust standard errors clustered by committee; our findings are presented in table 5.4. Our dependent variable is the percentage of LLBC-sponsored bills that died in committee over the four sessions. In the analysis, we only include committees that received at least one bill from a LLBC sponsor. Over the four sessions, 17 committees (14%) did not deal with any legislation sponsored by LLBC members. Our primary independent variables are the composition of the committees and the group identification of the committee chairs and vice-chairs. If members of the LLBC do not have strong legislative alliances with white Democrats and Republicans, then we would expect to find that more of their legislation died in committees chaired by white Democrats and Republicans and in those with fewer LLBC members. We also include the percentage of the committee bills that were black-interest bills in order to test whether it is the sponsor or the policy of the legislation that is important in this process. We include controls for session and chamber. Finally, we also control for the percentage of legislation that died in committee to determine whether some committees are more likely to stop all legislation, and not just that introduced by LLBC members.

Table 5.4 shows that bills sponsored by LLBC members were much less likely to die in committees with a black chair and more likely to die in committees with an overall higher rate of killing legislation. It is noteworthy that none of the other key variables reached statistical significance. Committees with a Democratic majority were not less likely to stop LLBC legislation than those controlled by Republicans. This reinforces our findings up to this point that the white Democrats do not spend a lot of time working with their LLBC counterparts. Therefore, LLBC members are not better

TABLE 5.4. Estimates for a Bill Dying in Committee

Variable	Model Estimates
LLBC chairmanship[a]	-19.1 (6.515)**
Republican chairmanship[a]	3.910 (5.392)
LLBC vice-chairmanship[b]	-5.50 (6.413)
Republican vice-chairmanship[b]	-8.14 (4.925)
% of LLBC members on committee	-.074 (.2015)
Democratic majority on committee	-1.98 (5.166)
% of black-interest bills	-.041 (.0694)
Chamber	-2.49 (4.589)
% of all bills that died in committee	.8113 (.1283)***
2005 special session[c]	4.262 (6.029)
2006 special session[c]	9.892 (7.746)
2006 regular session[c]	10.59 (4.959)*
Constant	18.92 (12.09)
N	104
R^2	0.43

Note: OLS regression is clustered by committee. Each cell contains the coefficient estimate, with robust standard error in parentheses.

[a]White Democratic chairs are the base category.
[b]White Democratic vice-chairs are the base category.
[c]The 2005 regular session is the base category.

$*p < .05, **p < .01, ***p < .001$

off having their bills sent to one of the Democratic-controlled committees. Surprisingly, Democrats only controlled 65 percent of the committees despite their majority in both chambers.

Another important finding is that LLBC-sponsored legislation does not fare better when sent to a committee with a greater number of LLBC members, as the percentage of LLBC committee members is not statistically significant. Surprisingly, LLBC-sponsored bills sent to committees with a majority of LLBC members do not reach statistical significance either.

However, this may simply be a statistical artifact, since only two committees (or seven data points across the four chambers)[31] had a majority of LLBC members. In both the house and the senate, this was essentially the local-government committee. The title of the house committee is House Committee on Municipal, Parochial, and Cultural Affairs, while the senate committee is titled Senate Committee on Local and Municipal Affairs. In both committees, blacks make up more than 60 percent of the membership, while the mean is 23 percent across all committees, and 12 committees have no LLBC members.

Black members tend to serve on committees that deal with black-interest legislation, and this allows them to focus on the needs of their constituents.[32] Since many black members come from similar districts, this strategy for both policy and constituent specialization makes perfect sense. However, our results show that the concentration of black members on certain committees does not lead to better results. The key is to obtain the position of chair of the committee. It is clearly important for the LLBC to place members in leadership positions in order to help further the agenda of black members. It is not enough to have members sit on similar committees; they need to become committee chairs. The power that comes from running a committee parlays into the ability to help steer a bill out of committee and in the direction of becoming law.

The LLBC Agenda

Our final examination of bill passage focuses on the LLBC's legislative agenda for the 2006 regular session. At the beginning of the 2006 regular session, the caucus published a legislative packet detailing the group's agenda for the session. The packet highlighted 54 bills that were a legislative priority for the caucus during the session. These bills constituted just 1 percent of the total bills introduced by black members during the session. This small percentage reinforces previous research findings stating that state legislative black caucuses "may take on a limited and manageable number of legislative initiatives in any one session."[33] By focusing on this agenda, we are able to compare the passage rates of bills that were a caucus priority with those introduced by black members that were not a formal caucus priority.

TABLE 5.5. The LLBC Agenda and Bill Outcomes

	Bills on LLBC Agenda % (No.)	Bills Not on LLBC Agenda % (No.)
Died in committee	47.17 (25)	50.60 (251)
Died on floor	18.87 (10)	19.35 (96)
Failed roll-call vote	13.21 (7)	1.61 (8)
Became law	33.96 (18)	30.04 (149)
Total votes	53	496

Note: "Failed roll-call vote" is a subset of the "died on floor" category. The total votes are calculated from the votes in the three main categories.

Table 5.5 shows very similar patterns for bills on the agenda and those not on the agenda. The findings suggest some caucus influence, as 34 percent of bills on the agenda became law, compared with only 30 percent of bills not on the agenda but introduced by black members. However, none of the results in the table reaches statistical significance in a t-test analysis. We also found that of the 10 bills on the agenda that died on the floor, 7 failed a roll-call vote. This is an extremely high number, considering that only 41 bills of nearly 2,300 introduced during the session died due to a roll-call vote. Of the 96 bills that died on the floor that were not on the agenda, only 8 failed a roll-call vote. LLBC members introduced 37 percent of all bills that were defeated by a roll-call vote.

Many of the bills in the packet were highly controversial. For example, there was a bill to reduce prison time for heroin possession, and others dealt with voting rights for displaced citizens of New Orleans after Hurricane Katrina. Overall, the LLBC focused on some of the most controversial issues facing the legislature, and gained slightly more victories than in the case of bills not endorsed by the caucus. Still, as discussed in the next chapter, the LLBC also endured some bitter failures.

Conclusion

One clear finding emerges in this chapter: LLBC-sponsored legislation is less likely than other legislation to make it through the legislative process and become law. This finding speaks volumes about the struggles of black legislators in the state; however, there is more to the story. First, we found that LLBC-supported legislation was more likely to pass than bills sponsored by black members without the endorsement of the caucus. While this was not a huge difference, it is important to note, since the caucus tends to tackle the more controversial and visible issues during a session. This suggests the institutional power of the LLBC and shows that black members are able to organize and work within the system to gain policy benefits. Additionally, as black members work their way into leadership roles, especially on committees, they have more success in passing legislation. This suggests another strategy for the LLBC: along with bringing attention to bills through the caucus agenda, members can attempt to gain access to power through the committee system.

Perhaps more important, we found that black-interest legislation, at least as we broadly define it, was slightly more likely to gain passage than other legislation, controlling for other factors. Ironically, it was most likely to pass if sponsored by a Republican and much less likely to pass if sponsored by a member of the LLBC. This intriguing finding suggests that white legislators might not simply ignore issues of concern to the black community. Unfortunately, our findings do not show whether the black-interest bills passed into law were for positive or negative changes, but at least they reflect that white legislators were dealing with these issues and not simply voting them down because of connections to issues within the black community. Overall, this situation put members of the LLBC in a tough position: they have to offer their support for these bills to satisfy their constituents even if they did not sponsor them, but they then face the concern that they might not be as successful when introducing their own legislation.

As table 5.1 shows, LLBC members, white Democrats, and Republicans passed legislation in similar policy areas, and in general black-interest legislation fit into these mainstream areas of legislation, once again suggesting that legislators were not simply casting aside legislation that dealt with black interests. However, individual black members had a harder time passing their legislation, regardless of the policy area, than did white legislators. Furthermore, since LLBC members represented most of the black constituents in the state, black legislators and constituents faced a disadvantage when striving for policy representation.

A second important finding also emerges in this chapter: the disadvantages faced by members representing New Orleans. This regional bias compounded the problems facing the LLBC in passing legislation. This was especially troubling for constituents, particularly black constituents in New Orleans, since 35 percent of the LLBC members represented some part of Orleans Parish, compared with just 7 percent of white Democrats and 9 percent of Republican members. This is crucial in a post-Katrina Louisiana, since a decline in the New Orleans population will more than likely lead to the loss of districts in redistricting and shift the power even further away from these members. As it stands now, white legislators from outside New Orleans are the most successful when passing legislation, and this should only strengthen, as the Orleans delegation will probably lose even more seats in the legislature.

Clearly, black members face an uphill battle in successfully navigating through the legislative maze. However, all is not lost for substantive representation of black issues. We found that LLBC members can increase their policy success by moving into committee leadership positions and by supporting black-interest legislation introduced by both white Democrats and Republicans.

6

Voting Cohesion, Ideology, and Coalitions

In December 2006, Governor Kathleen Blanco was desperately seeking legislative coalitions to support her $2.1 billion legislative package of new spending proposals and tax cuts, but the house was stuck in a stalemate of uncompromising groups. To grasp the reasons for this logjam, it is important to understand the meeting patterns of legislators during adjournment from their floor duties as "the Republican, Democratic, and Black caucuses huddled separately behind closed doors to debate strategy and search for solutions."[1] While this legislative defeat further eroded Governor Blanco's political capital, it also highlights an important strategic point: the Black Caucus met separately from the Democrats. Was this the normal operating procedure in the legislature? To answer this question, let us return to the bills introduced in chapter 5.

On the final and losing roll-call votes for allowing satellite voting locations for Katrina evacuees and for reducing the sentences for heroin possession, the members of the Black Caucus voted in lockstep for these bills, with the exception of one abstention on the voting bill. Meanwhile, their Republican colleagues voted in unison against the bills, with the exceptions of one abstention on the voting bill and one aye on the heroin-sentencing bill. In both cases the deciding votes were cast by white Democrats, enough of whom sided with the Republicans to swing the final outcome. Are these votes the exception or the norm? This will be the underlying question of this chapter as we examine several aspects of voting, from cohesion and ideology to the voting coalitions that determine the fate of legislation on both the house and senate floors.

Background on Voting in Minority Caucuses

The roll-call vote stands out as one of the most fundamental aspects of the legislative process. A representative boils down all of the complexities surrounding an issue into a binary vote either for or against a piece of legislation. While many of these votes occur without controversy, they provide much of the fodder for public examination of a legislator's record, and inside the chambers they tell the other members which legislators are with them and which are against them, so to speak. From these votes emerge patterns of cohesion and similarity among members and the coalitions for the compromise and logrolling of vote trading leading up to votes on the floor.

Given the reasons for forming black caucuses, along with the similarities between the constituencies of their members, most research, primarily at the congressional level, has found black caucuses to be cohesive units in the roll-call stage. Roxanne Gile and Charles E. Jones explored roll-call voting cohesion among members of the Congressional Black Caucus (CBC) from 1971 to 1995 and found the CBC to be a "highly cohesive" unit, especially in the area of social issues important to both their geographic and their national constituencies.[2] Similarly, Neil Pinney and George Serra found that members of the CBC voted more cohesively with the caucus than with representatives from either their states or their regions.[3] They argue that this cohesion helped the members pass policies important to the CBC. Marcus Pohlman suggests that a high level of cohesion gave the CBC bargaining power in the policy process, and Franklin Mixon and Rand Ressler argue that this voting cohesion allows the CBC to act as a cartel in the legislature, gaining CBC members positions on important committees in the Democratic Party because of their bargaining power.[4]

Not all scholars, however, agree with this assessment of cohesion among CBC members. Early on, Arthur Levy and Susan Stoudinger concluded that while the members of the CBC shared similar interests, the caucus "was not monolithic."[5] Controlling for seniority, they argued that freshman, junior, and senior members of Congress who belonged to the CBC voted in agreement less often with the caucus and more often with their state party delegations or with northern Democrats. More recently, Carol Swain has argued that members of the CBC vote together on issues such as civil rights, busing, and African policy but in general are not a cohesive group.[6] Particularly as the CBC membership has increased, it has had a harder time remaining unified, as members' home districts, committee interests, and political styles have become increasingly diverse.[7]

A series of articles on southern black legislative caucuses published in a special issue of the *Journal of Black Studies* in 2000 indicate that these caucuses had similar goals, their major goal being to pass legislation that was in the best interests of blacks by voting as a group on key legislation, specializing in and discussing important black issues, and disseminating information on these issues to the legislature and to the public. A similar sentiment emerged from journalistic coverage of the Maryland Black Caucus, with reports suggesting that revived leadership and group cohesion on key issues had helped the caucus to pass several important bills, such as a bill for the development of a system to deal with racial profiling in Maryland.[8]

However, several articles in the special issue concluded that black caucuses had not been particularly effective in meeting the important needs of the black population through voting cohesion. Robert Holmes concluded that the members of the Georgia Black Caucus had not been as successful as white members of the legislature in passing the legislation they sponsored; this was also the case in Mississippi.[9] Members of the Georgia Black Caucus were strong in their voting cohesion but were successful only after blacks became senior members in the legislature, gained key seats on committees, and established a good working relationship with the governor. Holmes concludes that the temptation to break from the caucus, which made the passage of legislation sponsored by caucus members more difficult, often became a reality "due to the [members'] tendency to promote themselves rather than the Caucus agenda."[10] Moreover, Holmes argues that a black caucus's involvement in an issue itself might hurt the chances of getting the issue passed, as the fact that a black representative sponsored it might mark the issue as a black issue.[11]

Analysis
Voting Cohesion

In order to measure the cohesiveness of the LLBC, we examine all the competitive roll-call votes from the 2005 and 2006 sessions. Here we define a competitive roll-call vote as one in which at least 5 percent of the chamber votes in the minority.[12] We use Stewart Rice's index of cohesion as our measure of cohesion.[13] This measure takes the absolute difference between the proportions of group (e.g., party or caucus) members voting yes and no. Thus, if all members vote with the majority of their party or caucus every time, then the group cohesion score is 1, and if the members vote against the majority of their group every time, the group cohesion score is 0.

As table 6.1 shows, the LLBC is the most cohesive group in both chambers of the Louisiana legislature. We include all of the regional and party caucuses, along with several informal groups (e.g., male and white Democrats). We average the cohesion scores across the four sessions and include both the percentage of one-party membership of a group (i.e., 1 if all members are Democrats or Republicans, 0.50 if there are equal numbers of Democrats and Republicans) and the average number of members (there were a few membership changes between sessions). Given the one-party nature of the LLBC and its relatively small membership, the high level of cohesion among its members should not be too surprising, because there is indeed a significant relationship between these two factors and cohesion.[14] These findings meet our expectations based on previous research and our interviews with LLBC members. While Louisiana has strong regional caucuses, membership in these caucuses represents an overlap in geography and not necessarily a policy focus. Without a doubt, as discussed in previous chapters, LLBC members represent demographically similar districts, and the group has a broader policy role beyond geography or demographics in bringing members together and promoting group cohesion.

Another way to think of cohesion is to look at the individual legislators and compare their scores with the average cohesion score for various groups. Using Rice's measure allows us to easily calculate the cohesiveness between any legislator and any group within the legislature. Tables 6.2 and 6.3 compare the cohesion of black and white members with the LLBC and other groups they belong to within the legislature. For the black members, the LLBC score represents the average cohesion of all the members of the group in column 1 with the caucus, and the "Other Caucus" score represents the average cohesion of the other groups to which they belong (the groups listed in column 1). The final column shows the number of

TABLE 6.1. Average Cohesion by Caucus or Group

Caucus or Group	Cohesion[a]	Partisanship[b]	Members[c]
House			
LLBC	0.68	1	22.75
Independent[d]	0.62	0.91	11
Jefferson	0.56	0.71	12.75
White Democrats[e]	0.57	1	40.25
Republican	0.55	1	41
Democratic	0.53	1	63
Acadiana	0.48	0.91	34
Orleans[d]	0.48	0.77	13
Women's	0.47	0.72	18
Rural[d]	0.47	0.71	65
Male[e]	0.43	0.68	87
Senate			
LLBC	0.72	1	9
Women's	0.66	0.74	6.75
Democratic	0.60	1	24
White Democrats[e]	0.60	1	15
Republican	0.56	1	14.75
Jefferson	0.54	0.53	5.75
Acadiana	0.53	0.69	13
Male[e]	0.44	0.59	32

[a] A cohesion score was calculated for each caucus in each session, and these scores were averaged across the 2005 and 2006 regular and special sessions. Higher numbers represent more cohesive voting among caucus or group members.
[b] Higher numbers represent a larger membership for one party. For example, a partisanship score of 1 indicates that all members belonged to the same party, while a score of .5 represents an even split between parties in the caucus or group.
[c] Average number of members in the caucus or group for each session. Due to retirements and special elections, there was some variation in the number of members per group across the four sessions.
[d] There were no senate members in the Independent and Orleans caucuses and only one in the Rural Caucus.
[e] Not an official caucus.

TABLE 6.2. Individual Membership Cohesion, House

Caucus or Group	LLBC	Other Caucus	N
Black Members			
Democratic	0.83	0.77	91
Rural	0.82	0.67	20
Women's	0.82	0.71	24
Orleans	0.85	0.84	28
Jefferson	0.84	0.53	3
Independent	0.85	0.77	4
Acadiana	0.79	0.71	20
White Members			
Democratic	0.67	0.78	157
Republican	0.46	0.78	164
Rural	0.56	0.74	236
Women's	0.59	0.73	48
Orleans	0.56	0.60	24
Jefferson	0.53	0.78	48
Independent	0.68	0.80	40
Acadiana	0.59	0.73	112

observations. The table compares all groups in which there was overlapping membership for black members and the LLBC. Since there were no black Republicans, we cannot compare those two groups. We assume that white members were part of the LLBC and calculate their cohesion with the caucus, along with their cohesion with the other groups to which they belonged.

An example from table 6.2 should help clarify these results: Looking at the first row, labeled "Democratic," under the heading "Black Members," we see that there were 91 legislators (over the four sessions, which means that in most cases an individual appears four times) that were members of both the LLBC and the Democratic Caucus. These 91 members showed more cohesion with the LLBC than with the Democratic Party (.83 to .77).

TABLE 6.3. Individual Membership Cohesion, Senate

Caucus or Group	LLBC	Other Caucus	N
	Black Members		
Democratic	0.85	0.81	16
Women's	0.86	0.87	16
Orleans	0.85	0.84	16
Jefferson	0.81	0.64	4
Acadiana	0.78	0.75	4
	White Members		
Democratic	0.71	0.78	60
Republican	0.51	0.76	59
Women's	0.65	0.72	11
Orleans	0.62	0.68	11
Jefferson	0.63	0.73	19
Acadiana	0.66	0.75	48

In other words, individuals who were members of both the LLBC and the Democratic Party tended to vote with the majority of LLBC members more often than they voted with Democrats.

This was a consistent theme for black legislators across chambers. Starting with the house in table 6.2, they showed more cohesion with the LLBC than with any other formal group with which they caucused in the legislature. The one exception was the Orleans Caucus, where the seven legislators (28 total across the four sessions) showed almost equally high levels of cohesion with both the LLBC (.85) and the entire Orleans Caucus (.84).

The bottom half of table 6.2 looks at voting cohesion among white legislators. Here the LLBC column shows the average cohesion score for white members with the majority of the LLBC, and the third column shows their cohesion with other caucuses to which they belonged. Here we find that white members were much more likely to vote with the caucus they belonged to than with the LLBC. In all cases except one we find at least a 10-point gap between the two scores. The largest gap, not surprisingly, is between the Republicans and the LLBC (.32), and the smallest is between the Orleans Caucus and the LLBC (.04).

Table 6.3 looks at the senate and shows a slightly different pattern. First, looking at the black members, we find cohesion scores for the individual members and the LLBC similar to those in the house. However, these senate members showed more cohesion with the other groups they belonged to than did their house counterparts. For each group, the black senators showed more or equal cohesion with their other groups than did their house counterparts, with the largest difference being in the Women's Caucus (.87 in the senate and .71 in the house). More importantly, we find that black female senators voted with the Women's Caucus slightly more than with the LLBC (.87 to .86). Additionally, for the members of the other groups, there was less difference between the LLBC and those groups in the senate, with the exception of the Orleans Caucus, which had equal cohesion-level differences in both chambers.

For the white senate members, we find very similar patterns to those in the house, with all members voting more with the groups to which they belonged than with the LLBC. As in the house, the smallest difference was in the Orleans Caucus (.06). This tells us that the voting pattern of members of the Orleans Caucus, regardless of race, was similar to that of LLBC members. This finding fits with our discussions in the earlier chapters, which highlight the similarities in the agenda, vote outcomes, and demographics of the two groups.

Overall, the LLBC was the most cohesive group in the Louisiana legislature, and its members showed the greatest difference between their cohesiveness with the LLBC and their cohesiveness with other groups to which they belonged. The one exception in the house was the Orleans Caucus, which showed no difference, and the one exception in the senate was the Women's Caucus, whose four black female senators were actually more likely to vote along gender rather than racial lines, although this was only a 1 percent difference. While the LLBC was more cohesive in the upper chamber (.72 to .66), individual house members showed more cohesion with the LLBC than with the others groups to which they belonged. This analysis leaves little doubt that the LLBC provided its members a consistent voting bloc that was more reliable than both the party caucuses and the regional caucuses in the state. Across both chambers, only members of the Orleans Caucus, both black and white, showed levels of cohesion similar to those of LLBC members. This fits with the emerging story that race is a dividing line in the legislature, along with and tied into the "New Orleans versus the rest of the state" mentality prevalent throughout Louisiana politics and culture.[15]

Ideology

While the above analysis shows a strong cohesion among members of the LLBC, it does not tell us anything about the ideological slant of their voting patterns. The common view of legislative voting in the U.S. Congress is one of a unidimensional structure that reflects the liberal-conservative, or left-right, ideological continuum.[16] Despite a recent debate in the political science literature, it is clear that one of the key factors in this unidimensional structure is the role of strong political parties.[17] The parties work toward voting outcomes based on their ideology and provide structure to the voting patterns of their members. Without strong parties, this structure would break down, leaving little framework to guide members' voting decisions.[18]

While Congress has demonstrated a generally stable voting structure based on ideology, there is some evidence that parties are not always as strong in some state legislatures, allowing a second dimension of voting to influence outcomes.[19] Initial studies suggest that factors ranging from race, constituency diversity, and affiliations with regional and issue caucuses to procedural rules can form important second dimensions of roll-call voting. It is worth noting that in each of these studies, party and ideology remains the most important dimension, even with the aforementioned second-dimension factors adding a smaller but important structure to roll-call voting.

Using methods common in this line of research, we examine the voting patterns in the Louisiana legislature using W-NOMINATE scores.[20] Essentially, we compute a score for each legislator based on his or her voting patterns, and from these patterns emerges a dimensionality for the overall structure of roll-call voting in each chamber. We assume that this dimensionality represents the ideological continuum from conservative to liberal. We show this continuum in figures 6.1 and 6.2 by plotting scores ranging from -1 (most conservative) to 1 (most liberal) on the x-axis, along with the unidentified second dimension on the y-axis. It is worth noting that this *conservative/liberal* terminology applies to the respective chambers only. We cannot assume that *liberal* and *conservative* mean the same thing in Louisiana that they do in other states or even that they mean the same thing in both chambers of the Louisiana legislature.

Figures 6.1 and 6.2 illustrate the dimensionality of the 2005 and 2006 regular sessions for the house and the senate, respectively.[21] Figure 6.1 plots the W-NOMINATE scores for each member of the house by group affiliation in the 2005 and 2006 regular sessions. We notice several important features of the voting patterns. First, LLBC members were generally the most liberal in the chamber, the majority of them clustering between .5 and 1 on the first dimension. The remaining members of the LLBC cluster alongside white Democrats but were more liberal than most white Democrats and all of the Republicans. Second, the Republicans were clearly the most conservative, with most members between -.5 and -1 on the first dimension. Most white Democrats were in the middle of the spectrum (between -.25 and .5) along with several small groups of Republicans. A similar pattern emerges for the 2006 regular session, with members of the LLBC the most liberal and Republicans the most conservative. Once again,

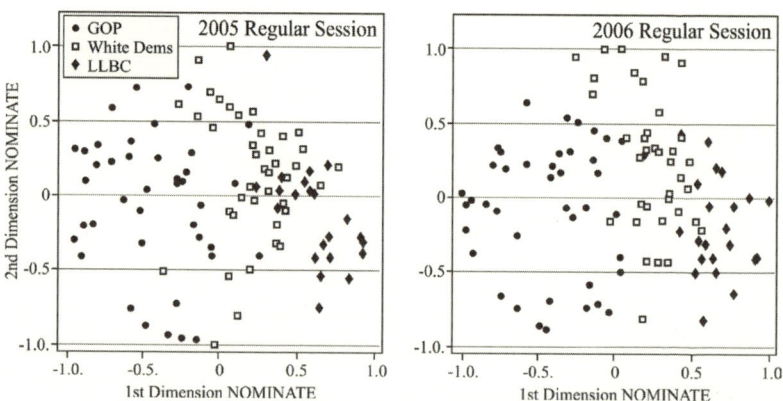

FIGURE 6.1. Roll-Call Voting by Group in the House, 2005 and 2006 Regular Sessions

Voting Cohesion, Ideology, and Coalitions

the white Democrats fit a moderate profile, exhibiting some overlap with both Republicans and members of the LLBC.

Turning to the senate, figure 6.2 shows a clear delineation between liberal and conservative senators. We see very few senators in the moderate range (around the 0 mark), with most falling along party lines to the extremes. Members of the LLBC were the most liberal, with only one member of the caucus less liberal than any of the white Democrats. Interestingly, white Democrats were essentially split between their liberal and conservative wings, with each having seven members on each side of the aisle and one moderate member in the middle of the spectrum. The Republicans were quite cohesive along the conservative side of the spectrum, with one outlier clustered in with the liberal white Democrats. There was a similar pattern in the 2006 regular session, but with a little more moderation across the chamber. The members of the LLBC remained the most liberal, but several members moved slightly to the right in terms of ideology. The white Democrats were still more conservative, but the most conservative members moved more toward the middle. The Republicans remained clearly conservative, with their one outlier member moderating more toward the middle of the ideological spectrum.

Overall, we find that the LLBC was consistently the most liberal group in the legislature, as well as the most cohesive. What drove this ideological consistency? To answer this question, we model different factors that

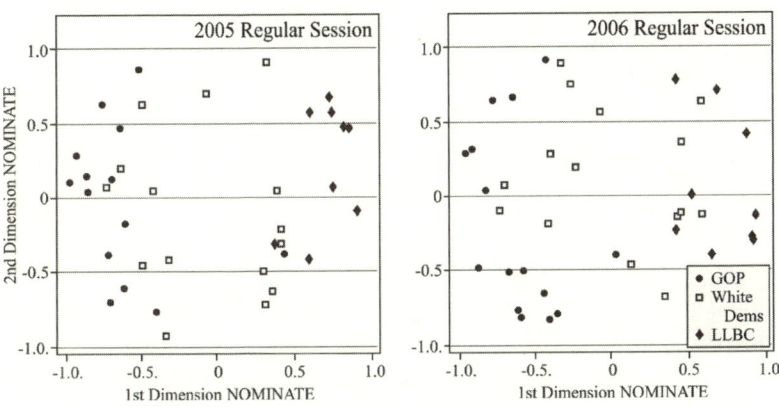

FIGURE 6.2. Roll-Call Voting by Group in the Senate, 2005 and 2006 Regular Sessions

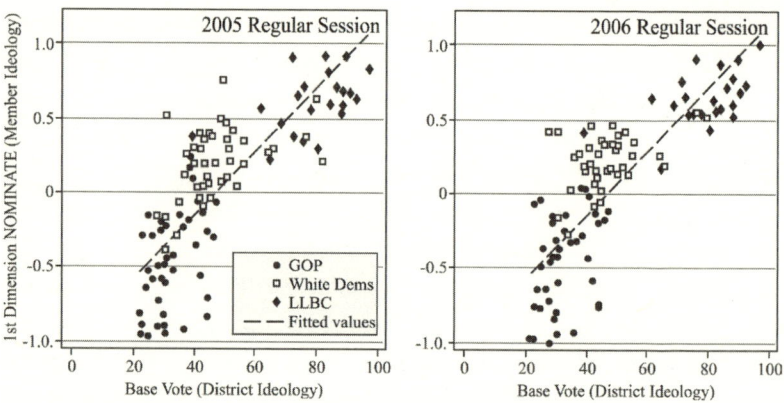

FIGURE 6.3. Roll-Call Voting and Constituency Influence in the House, 2005 and 2006 Regular Sessions

often drive legislative behavior. The one factor that stands out is district partisanship. Using the 2000 presidential vote as a proxy for underlying district partisanship, it is clear that most legislators voted in response to constituency preferences.[22] In figures 6.3 and 6.4, we present scatter plots for the 2005 and 2006 regular sessions capturing this effect, along with the fitted line from our model with the first-dimension NOMINATE scores on the vertical axis and the base vote (the percentage voting for Gore by district) along the horizontal axis.[23]

Several important findings emerge in figure 6.3. First, we see that members of the LLBC represented the most liberal districts, which, as discussed in chapter 3, were all majority-black districts. Second, the Republicans represented, with few exceptions, the most conservative districts and fall below the fitted line. The white Democrats generally represented moderate districts (mean Gore vote = .47), with a few representing more Democratic districts and a handful representing districts that supported Gore at below 30 percent. Finally, we can see the pull of party, as most Republicans fall below the fitted line, and most white Democrats fall above the line, indicating that while constituency has a major influence on voting, it is not the only factor, as party also has an important institutional role. Figure 6.4 shows a similar pattern in the senate. One important difference is the larger gap along the ideological dimension for the white Democrats. While most white Democrats

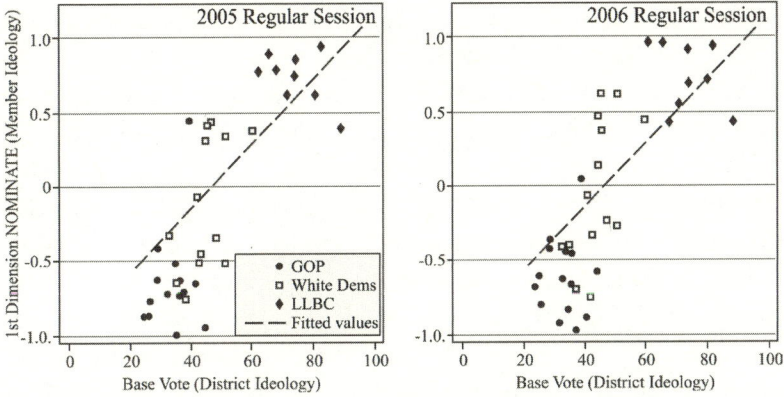

FIGURE 6.4. Roll-Call Voting and Constituency Influence in the Senate, 2005 and 2006 Regular Sessions

represented districts with similar partisanship, there was a divide between those who fall above and below the fitted line. The white senate Democrats appear to have been more divided than their house counterparts.

Overall, we see the importance of constituency in the representational relationship, as members from the most conservative or Republican districts were not only Republican but also had the most conservative voting records. Conversely, the LLBC members from the most Democratic districts, which also happen to be majority black, had the most liberal voting records. Finally, the white Democrats represented the moderate districts and had moderate voting records. More important, the white Democrats from the most Republican-leaning districts had the most conservative voting records among the group, while white Democrats from more Democratic-leaning districts voted more liberally. Discussing the role of constituency helps us to better understand the ideological voting patterns, but it does not tell us how successful these groups are in getting their preferred outcomes on roll-call votes.

Coalitions

Turning back to our two examples at the beginning of the chapter, we end our analysis with a look at the voting coalitions formed in the chambers. We know that the LLBC is the most cohesive and the most liberal group in the legislature. This would seem to limit their coalition-building partners to the more liberal white Democrats.

A look at the numbers in the legislature shows the challenge that members of the LLBC faced in forging winning coalitions. Starting with the house, during the 2006 regular session the Democrats held 63 seats, while the Republicans had only had 41, and there was 1 independent. With 60 percent of the seats, the Democrats held a relatively safe margin and a 10-vote cushion on most votes in the legislature. Within the Democratic majority, the LLBC held 23 seats, which left white Democrats with 40 seats, or one less than the Republicans. Thus, the white Democrats needed to pick up 13 votes to have a majority, while the Republicans needed 12. In the senate, the Democrats held 24 of the 39 seats, or 61 percent, and of those 24 seats, LLBC members occupied 9. This left 15 white Democrats and 15 Republicans, who only needed to gain 5 votes to secure a majority on a bill. Interestingly, in both chambers the LLBC gave majority-party status to the Democrats. But was this a significant factor in winning roll-call votes, or did the white Democrats simply work across the aisle with the Republicans instead of within their own party?

To get an idea of the coalition structure within the chambers, we start by examining our ideological measure, first-dimension NOMINATE, to determine the voting overlap among the groups. We use a box and whisker plot as a visual reference. In each box the white line represents the median, or the middle 50 percent of the data. The upper and lower hinges of the

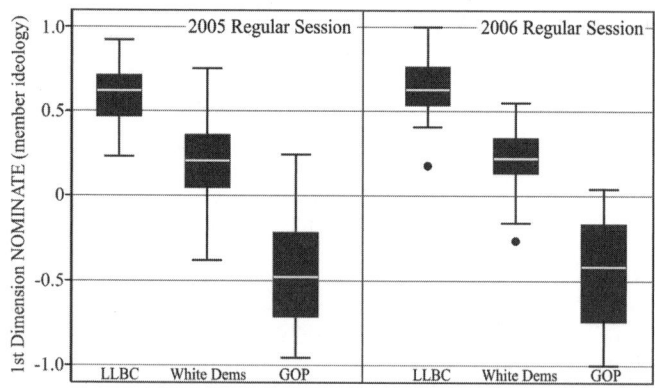

FIGURE 6.5. Voting Coalitions in the House, 2005 and 2006 Regular Sessions

Voting Cohesion, Ideology, and Coalitions

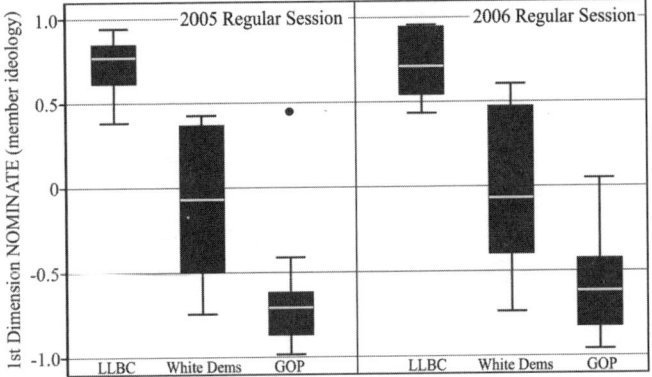

FIGURE 6.6. Voting Coalitions in the Senate, 2005 and 2006 Regular Sessions

boxes show, respectively, the 75th percentile, or third quartile, and the 25th percentile, or first quartile. Each box also represents the interquartile range (IQR), which is the difference between the first and third quartiles. The whiskers extend to 1.5 times beyond the interquartile range; in the cases where the data do not extend that far, the whiskers are the minimum and maximum values. Any data point that is more than 1.5 times the IQR shows up as outliers beyond the whiskers.

Figures 6.5 and 6.6 show box plots for the house and the senate, respectively, during the 2005 and 2006 regular sessions. Starting with the house, figure 6.5 shows very little overlap between the groups in either session, with none of the boxes overlapping. For neither session does the IQR of one group overlap with that of any other group. For the 2005 session, the whiskers of the white Democrats overlap with the IQRs of both the LLBC and the Republicans, with the LLBC and GOP whiskers also overlapping with the IQR of the white Democrats. In 2006, the ideological distinction was even greater. The only overlap is between the whiskers of the LLBC and those of the most liberal white Democrats, and this overlap pertains to the most conservative white Democrats and the most moderate Republicans. Thus, the three groups are basically ideologically distinct voting blocs with no significant ideological overlap between most of each group's members. This lack of overlap does not point to a clear winning coalition. However, the average white Democratic member was closer to the average LLBC member than to the Republicans. While this is not strong evidence, it does suggest that the white Democrats as a group were more ideologically aligned with the LLBC than with the Republicans. However, some research suggests that much of the party agreement may be a result of procedural and not substantive votes.[24]

Figure 6.6 shows a similar pattern in the senate, with two notable exceptions. First, the white Democrats' IQR is much larger. This tells us that there was greater ideological diversity among the 15 white Democrats in the senate than among the 40 white Democrats in the house. More important, the median white Democrat in the senate was more conservative and closer to the Republican's median member. Thus, the white Democrats in the senate were more ideologically aligned with the GOP than with the LLBC, suggesting that it was more difficult for senate LLBC members to get the votes they needed for a majority coalition.

Table 6.4 shows the makeup of winning coalitions in order to see whether the LLBC was able to work with the white Democrats and even across the aisle with Republicans. The table presents a pairwise comparison of the three groups, showing how often a majority of the members in each group voted together on the winning side of a roll-call vote. We code a winning coalition for a bill when the majority of one group's members voted with the majority of another group's members and the bill could not have passed without any support from the third group. In other words, this table shows the percentage of legislation that could have passed with only the support of the majorities of two groups, that is, with no support from the third group. This helps account for the most competitive voting situations in the legislature, not those in which the three groups were in general agreement with one another.

The white Democrats were in the driver's seat in the Louisiana legislature, working with both the LLBC and Republicans to pass legislation. In fact, they tended to work with the GOP more often than with the LLBC. In both the house and the senate, the white Democrats formed successful coalitions with the Republicans between 25 percent and 28 percent of the time, while they formed successful coalitions with the LLBC only between 5 percent and 10 percent of the time. The LLBC and the Republicans never formed a successful coalition.

Table 6.5 shows how often a group achieved its desired outcome, by chamber for the 2005 and 2006 regular sessions. We define a vote as a

Voting Cohesion, Ideology, and Coalitions

TABLE 6.4. Voting Coalitions

	House		Senate	
	2005	2006	2005	2006
LLBC–White Democrats	9.09 (18)	10.37 (39)	8.26 (10)	5.00 (11)
White Democrats–Republicans	25.76 (51)	25.80 (97)	28.10 (34)	28.64 (63)
LLBC-Republicans	0 (0)	0 (0)	0 (0)	0 (0)
Total votes	198	376	121	220

Note: Each cell contains the percentage of votes in which a bill passed with support from only the majority of each group, with total votes in parentheses.

"win" for a group when the final vote reflected the votes of the majority of the group's members. For example, the two bills presented at the beginning of this chapter are not coded as "wins" for the LLBC, since while the majority of the LLBC voted in favor of the bills, they did not pass. Table 6.5 also shows the likelihood of a group's winning based on the outcome of the other groups' voting fortunes.

Looking first at the overall numbers, we see that the white Democrats achieved their desired outcome more than 90 percent of the time in both chambers. Beyond that, we see some important chamber differences. In the house, the LLBC won 77 percent of all votes, well above the GOP's 63.76 percent. However, in the senate the Republicans were slightly more successful than the LLBC (77.13% to 76.25%). Party was more influential in the house, as both the white Democrats and the LLBC were more successful in achieving their desired outcome. In the senate, however, party was less influential, as the GOP was just as successful as the LLBC. The fact that the Republicans were just as successful as the LLBC is not surprising in light of figures 6.5 and 6.6, which show the median white Democrat ideologically closer to the median Republican member than to the median LLBC member.

Table 6.5 also shows a group's wins in the context of the outcomes for other groups as another way to assess the role of coalitions in voting. We find that in both chambers the LLBC was most successful when the Republicans lost (95.67% of the time in the house and 100% in the senate) and when the white Democrats won (82.22% of the time in the house and 79.98% in the senate). Both results highlight the importance of party for the LLBC members, who had to work with their Democratic partners to achieve policy success, and were most successful when the majority of Republicans opposed their stance. This is not surprising given the ideological slant of the LLBC members and their cohesiveness. They represented the extremes of the Democratic Party and had to look for support from moderate Democrats to gain a majority.

The LLBC was least successful when the white Democrats lost (26% of the time in the house and 44.44% in the senate). The fact that LLBC members only achieved their desired outcome 26 percent of the time when a majority of white Democrats voted against them in the house shows that the LLBC was not very successful when it had to piece together a nonmajority coalition of white Democrats. In the senate, the LLBC was more successful when the majority of white Democrats voted against them, but even then the success rate was less than 50 percent.

Tables 6.4 and 6.5 illustrate the inability of the LLBC and the GOP to work together. Specifically, in the house the Republicans had a success rate of 93.18 percent when a majority of the LLBC voted against them, and the LLBC members had a 95.67 percent success rate when a majority of Republicans voted against them. In the senate, this occurred 100 percent of the time for both groups. It is clear that these two groups did not support the same issues. This was due not only to party but also to ideology and constituency differences between the groups' members.

The LLBC was most successful when working within the Democratic Party. It could not or did not form coalitions across the partisan aisle, even though there were the same number of white Democrats as Republicans in both chambers. This was partly due to numbers, as the white Democrats had more Republicans to work with in creating majorities. However, we would expect party label to have had a stronger pull, with the Democrats working together, but this does not appear to have been the case, especially in the senate. From a constituency perspective, however, this outcome may not be very surprising, as figures 6.3 and 6.4 clearly show that most white

TABLE 6.5. Winning Policy Support, 2005 and 2006 Regular Sessions

Win	Overall % (No.)	GOP Win % (No.)	GOP Loss % (No.)	Group Position LLBC Win % (No.)	LLBC Loss % (No.)	WD[a] Win % (No.)	WD[a] Loss % (No.)
				House			
GOP	63.76 (366)	—	—	54.88 (242)	93.23 (124)	60.69 (318)	96.0 (48)
LLBC	76.83 (441)	66.12 (242)	95.67 (199)	—	—	81.68 (428)	26.00 (13)
WD[a]	91.29 (524)	86.89 (318)	99.04 (206)	97.05 (428)	72.18 (96)	—	—
				Senate			
GOP	77.13 (263)	—	—	70.00 (182)	100 (81)	76.43 (240)	85.19 (23)
LLBC	76.25 (260)	69.20 (182)	100 (78)	—	—	79.98 (248)	44.44 (12)
WD[a]	92.08 (314)	91.25 (240)	94.87 (74)	95.38 (248)	81.48 (66)	—	—

[a] White Democrats

Democrats represented districts with partisanship closer to that of most Republicans' districts than to that of LLBC members' districts. Finally, white Democrats were in the best position to achieve policy success. They not only had majority status, as they could work strategically with the LLBC when necessary, but they also represented constituencies similar to those of many Republicans. Thus, they could use constituency similarities to their benefit when building support for their policies. The LLBC was an important part of the white Democrats' policy success, as they were least successful when a majority of the LLBC voted against them (70.45% of the time in the house and 81.48% in the senate). These percentages also highlight the fundamental limitation of the LLBC as a major force in successful coalition building. The LLBC was not large enough and was not similar enough to the white Democrats in terms of ideology and constituency to wield sufficient power to stop proposals they opposed.

Conclusion

The LLBC possessed both advantages and disadvantages for securing public policy for its constituents during the 2005 and 2006 legislative sessions. On the plus side, the LLBC was the most cohesive group in the legislature. LLBC members voted together more often than any other regional or minority caucus, even more than members of the two parties. In part, this cohesion clearly stemmed not only from sharing a party label but also from representing similar districts. This cohesion provided the LLBC with support for advocating public policy and led to a tight-knit voting network.

This cohesion was important since all members of the LLBC were Democrats and they were in the majority in both chambers. However, the pull of party appears to have given the LLBC an advantage only in the house and not in the senate. In the house, being in the majority allowed the LLBC and the Democrats as a whole to win more often than the Republicans on roll-call votes. In the senate, however, the GOP was just as successful as the LLBC in winning its desired outcome as a group.

The negatives tended to outweigh the positives, however, as the LLBC faced several critical obstacles in trying to gain its policy objectives. The first was simply the numbers: while the LLBC was one of the largest

Voting Cohesion, Ideology, and Coalitions

black caucuses in the country, black legislators only made up roughly 20 percent of the legislature. This meant that the white Democrats had more Republicans than LLBC members to work with when building coalitions. In addition, in many ways the fact that the LLBC was not only the most cohesive but also the most liberal group in the legislature isolated the LLBC from the rest of the legislators, whose voting patterns were more moderate or conservative. Therefore, when coalitions formed on a roll-call vote, most white Democrats were likely to vote with members who shared a similar ideology, and this happened to be the Republicans rather than the LLBC.

Finally, due to majority-minority districting, the districts represented by LLBC members, which were not only majority-black districts but also the most Democratic, were distinctly different from those represented by the other legislators. Once again, most white Democrats represented districts whose constituents' partisanship was closer to that of the Republicans than to that of the LLBC. When the white Democrats voted in response to the pull of their constituency, they often cast votes similar to those cast by the Republicans and not to those cast by the LLBC. In this book's concluding chapter, we come back to these issues to discuss strategies by which the LLBC can achieve more policy success.

Conclusion

The Louisiana Legislative Black Caucus was formed in 1977 to lead the charge in providing representation to blacks in the legislative arena. Since its inception, we have seen an increase in the number of black legislators in the Louisiana legislature; however, according to many socioeconomic indicators, the condition of blacks in Louisiana has not improved. In our examination of the role of the LLBC, along with its successes and failures in the legislative arena, we discovered a great deal. For example the LLBC agenda is similar to the agendas of both Republicans and white Democrats, although the LLBC's is more likely to be geared toward black-interest legislation. LLBC members vote together more often than do the members of any other group in the legislature, with a few exceptions. And members of the LLBC have the lowest bill-passage rates; however, at the committee level, LLBC chairs pass a higher percentage of LLBC-sponsored legislation.

There are many ways to measure legislative successes and failures. One of the most obvious ways is to measure bill-passage rates. We found that of all the groups we analyzed, the LLBC had the lowest bill-passage rates. Why would this be the case if Democrats (of which LLBC members were a part) were in the majority in the Louisiana legislature? We would expect the LLBC to have been somewhat more successful than the minority Republicans. One of the main reasons for the LLBC's low bill-passage rates (as we established from the interviews) was the inability of the LLBC to form coalitions across party lines and even at times within their own party. Other factors worked against the LLBC's policy success, most notably their voting ideology and the districts they represented. The LLBC represented the most liberal districts in the state, as well as all the majority-minority districts. To accurately represent their constituents, the LLBC must stake out positions that do not overlap with those of many other legislators from either party throughout the state. As a result of the districting process, most white Democrats represent districts more closely aligned with their Republican colleagues than with the LLBC. This is a tough representational threshold to cross when trying to build strong and lasting voting coalitions. This finding helps to explain why the conditions remain the same for blacks in Louisiana: the policies offered by the LLBC members (which target specific issues faced by their constituents) often fail to garner enough support to pass. This leads us to ask whether the caucus is effective.

Is the Caucus Effective?

It is difficult to take a definitive position on the effectiveness of the caucus, since how one defines *effective* depends on one's perspective. We believe the LLBC is effective in terms of descriptive representation, meaning that the LLBC's mere presence in the legislature creates an opportunity for its members to share their perspectives, opinions, and interests during the legislative process. We see clear evidence of this not only in the number but also in the types of bills introduced by LLBC members. Without their presence in the deliberative process, while the broad policy topics might be very similar, the specifics of the bills might be very different. For example, in the 24th Judicial District Court, in Jefferson Parish (just outside New Orleans), there are sixteen judges, with two blacks elected from majority-black districts. Two members of the Louisiana legislature (both black) introduced a bill to increase the number of black judges from two to three. Their rationale for proposing the bill was that Jefferson Parish was 31 percent black and needed additional representation on the judiciary. In this case (and in many similar cases), the LLBC proposed a bill that its white counterparts (both Democrats and Republicans) might not have proposed. As stated earlier, descriptive representation entails not only offering bills but also having a seat at the table, so that everyone's opinions can be expressed well before bills are brought to committee. Our conversations with LLBC members revealed that their participation in informal and formal discussions on policy matters is widespread. At the invitation of one of the members of the LLBC, one of us was able to sit in on a meeting with the governor's chief of staff and legal team as they discussed with a member of the LLBC a whole host of policy issues and asked whether they could count on this member's support. As they presented their ideas for specific bills, the black legislator asked questions and discussed their proposals with them, at the very least providing a differing perspective on the issues.

Overall, the members of the LLBC identify with the black community and share similar views toward racial identity and the place of blacks in the American political system. These similar viewpoints provide the members a common base from which to represent their constituents and work together in the legislature. However, we also know that outside of race, LLBC members do not share many characteristics with their average constituents. Members of the LLBC are wealthier and better educated than their constituents; in fact, LLBC members have more in common, at least from a socioeconomic perspective, with their white Democratic and Republican colleagues. In addition to wealth and education, LLBC members share a common racial identity, and these commonalities should help the caucus work toward a shared vision of representing the black constituency within individual districts and the state as a whole.

Another way in which the LLBC members are effective descriptively is that their presence in the legislature constructs positive social meaning. Many of the black legislators whom we interviewed indicated that their constituents looked up to them and that their elected position offered hope to their constituents that they too might achieve success and even aspire to run for political office. One LLBC member stated that he had seen increased black interest in running for political office since blacks had been elected to the legislature. We can also gauge the descriptive effectiveness of LLBC members by considering the purpose of their organization. The major reason for its foundation was to intercede and bridge the communication gap between government and blacks. Most members we interviewed indicated they were very active in their districts, holding town-hall meetings, meeting with constituents one on one, and sending out newsletters to report on policy discussions and outcomes. In this respect, the LLBC has been effective in terms of descriptive representation.

On the other hand, our findings indicate that the LLBC members have been less effective in terms of substantive representation, that is, in enacting legislation that furthers the interests of the minority community. LLBC members' legislation was the most likely to be stopped in committee and the least likely to become law. Even a concentration of black members on certain committees did not ultimately lead to better results. The key was to obtain the chairmanship of committees, especially financial committees. We are not saying that LLBC members do not get bills passed in the legislature that help their constituents, but that their overall success rate is lower than that of the other legislators. For example, Republicans (who were in the minority in both chambers) have better success rates than black Democrats.

Factors Affecting Success Rates

Why do LLBC members have such a low level of success in getting legislation passed? First, maybe there is not the necessary level of communication between the LLBC and white Democrats. We found that white Democrats do not devote much time to working with their LLBC counterparts, and many of the LLBC members we interviewed were not happy with the Democratic Party organization. Some said that the Democratic Party took black members for granted; others claimed that the Democrats were not unified in terms of their priorities. For example, a couple of the LLBC members described the Democratic Party as weak. According to one interviewee, "The Democratic Party has always been in power, and there hasn't been that great deal of emphasis put on party." Another LLBC member told us, "I'd love to sit here and say we [the Democratic Party] have a unified agenda, but I can't honestly sit here and be truthful to you and say yes, we have a unified agenda." Even when there was an agenda, a member of the LLBC said, "The agenda of the Democratic Party is very splintered, and it really needs a lot of work" because "there are major philosophical differences between the LLBC and the Democratic Party." Based on these statements, it is not difficult to understand why the LLBC is often overlooked and why its legislative priorities are not supported by the white Democrats. There seems to be limited communication between the two groups, and even when there is interaction, it seems to reflect deep philosophical differences.

Second, many members said that there were obstacles to passing legislation, mainly racial prejudice. According to one member, while the white Democrats were friendly to LLBC members, it was a superficial friendliness; beneath it was a deep-seated view that the black members were intruding on their "white-boy fraternity." Another member said that "racial prejudices still exists and it's unfortunate . . . but we handle it by not talking down to anyone or try to incite fear in them, but try to basically massage them and educate them and sensitize them to the facts about the subject matter."

Many members argued that committee assignments hurt their ability to pass legislation. LLBC members indicated that they were usually appointed to the least powerful committees. If they held the post of chair or vice-chair of a committee, it was one of these least powerful committees. A member of the LLBC explained, "Typically, if you look at the makeup of the committees, most of the people that you'll see having influence over the money committees (i.e., Ways and Means committee, Appropriations committee) are all white males; black members are on Education, Municipal and Local Affairs Committees, and Criminal Justice Committees. So, committee structures are unequal."

The third possible explanation for LLBC members' low rate of success in passing legislation is the internal disagreements among members of the LLBC on policy and power. While many people view black politicians as extremely unified, and our results in chapter 6 suggest this, our interviews revealed that it is not always the case. There are major policy disagreements between black legislators representing northern Louisiana and those representing southern Louisiana, between black legislators representing New Orleans and those representing the rest of the state, and on moral issues.

In addition to differing policy differences (at least on some issues), there are internal disagreements regarding power. Several members indicated an internal struggle between members over the direction and leadership of the caucus. Debate and discussion are always good; however, division and grandstanding (for the purpose of fulfilling a personal agenda) can be destructive to any organization. In 2008 the LLBC chair, Juan LaFonta of New Orleans, announced that he would cut his term short because of disagreements over how to work with Governor Bobby Jindal. Some members of the caucus had accused LaFonta of being too cozy with the Republican governor and potentially selling out the group's agenda.[1] Thus, if the LLBC is to be more effective, it must deal with these issues. However, the reality is that "black legislators are in a double bind. Caught between pressures to represent blacks collectively as a holistic unit and constraints dictated by their individual political circumstances, they can neither act solely as a unit nor solely as an individual."[2]

Finally, we offer some possible reasons why the LLBC does not have more success in passing legislation. For one thing, there were only 32 LLBC members in the legislature, and there were not enough members in either chamber to either block legislation or effectively create coalitions that would lead to successful voting outcomes. Also, LLBC members may propose policies that white legislators cannot fully support either because of district concerns or because they are not relevant to their districts. Finally, it is possible that LLBC proposals are simply bad public policy. We doubt that this is usually the case, since our analysis shows that all legislators introduced and passed legislation in the same general policy areas. Whatever the ultimate explanation, even though the LLBC is a well-established organization, it still faces an uphill battle in passing substantive legislation.

Possible Ways to Increase Effectiveness

There are numerous ways in which the LLBC might increase policy effectiveness. The most obvious is to add more blacks to the Louisiana legislature. An increase in the number of LLBC members might increase the support for some of the policies offered by the LLBC. This might also force white Democrats and Republicans to work with members of the LLBC. However, increasing the number of blacks in the Louisiana legislature is going to be difficult unless blacks run and win in majority-white districts. A quick glance at the state's demographics suggests that adding additional majority-black districts is unlikely. In fact, the state may see one or two majority-blacks districts disappear because Hurricane Katrina has caused many blacks to leave New Orleans. Even more interesting is that white candidates have been winning in traditionally majority-black districts. At least two white legislators currently serving in the Louisiana house represent majority-black districts.

Thus, the LLBC may need to adopt a more campaign-oriented strategy to elect members in non-majority-minority districts. However, this will not be easy, as no black member of the Louisiana legislature has ever been elected from a majority-white district; furthermore, no black candidate requiring substantial white support has ever been elected to a statewide office. This is certainly not to say that a black candidate cannot win in a majority-white district; however, there are challenges. The elections of Barack Obama as president of the United States and of Bobby Jindal as governor of Louisiana give hope to minority candidates that they can win outside of majority-minority districts. However, we are not convinced that one presidential victory and one Republican gubernatorial victory have suddenly shifted the entire voting landscape in the United States, and we are certain that they have not in the Deep South.

This strategy described above may need to coincide with a shift in redistricting toward fewer majority-minority districts and more "influence" districts (35%–45% minority population). Such a shift, with well-funded and well-planned campaigns on the part of the Democratic Party, might increase the number of black members and might increase the Democrats' overall competitiveness. One possible concern for the LLBC is that a shift towards "influence" districts may lead to a larger proportion of black voters being represented by white legislators. How to handle a potential increase in the number of non-black legislators representing districts with significant black populations is an important question that all Democratic and black leaders in charge of redistricting must tackle, and it is one that is at the center of the discussion on descriptive representation.

Louisiana's representation in the U.S. Congress provides an excellent illustration. The Congressional Black Caucus refused membership to Anh "Joseph" Cao, a Republican of Vietnamese descent who represented New Orleans in the Second Congressional District. Cao sought membership in the CBC as a way to represent his majority-black district in New Orleans.[3] The CBC had never faced a situation of a non-black legislator representing a majority-black district until Cao's 2008 election and so far has shown little interest in diversifying its membership. If the LLBC hopes to increase its electoral and policy reach, it must consider opening its membership to others besides African Americans in the near future.

A reduction in the number of racially gerrymandered districts, issues of race in elections, and white candidates' success in majority-black districts do not bode well for the LLBC's ability to increase black representation in the Louisiana legislature using its current strategies. Nevertheless, the only electoral option that remains is for black candidates to continue to pursue campaigns in majority-white districts and develop winning strategies to increase their numbers.

Besides increasing their numbers, another possibility is for the LLBC to solidify its policy goals with those of white Democrats (or the Democratic Party organization). It seems that while there is informal discussion between black members and white Democrats, there is never a formal discussion between the LLBC and the Democratic leadership about the LLBC's priorities. Establishing such a dialogue before the legislative session begins might help white Democrats understand why the LLBC pushes certain policies. There seems to be no reason why the LLBC and white Democrats cannot come to a formal agreement on some of the policies offered by the LLBC.

If Republicans pass more legislation than the LLBC, and white Democrats tend to work with the GOP more often than the LLBC, then why are members of the LLBC part of the Democratic Party? One reason for belonging to a particular political party is to be able to utilize that party as a vehicle to pass legislation. For whatever reason, being part of the Democratic Party has not yielded a great deal of policy success for the LLBC. The LLBC needs to hold the Democratic Party accountable. If the Democratic Party does not support some of the policies offered by the LLBC (and would rather work with the Republican Party), then the caucus ought to signal to the Democratic leadership that it (while part of the Democratic Party) will act independently, regardless of the party's interests. In other words, the Democratic Party cannot assume that the LLBC will support all of its policy initiatives. The Democratic Party has been appeasing LLBC members by making them chairs and vice-chairs of the least influential committees in the legislature, and holding leadership positions in these committees has not increased their legislative success. We believe that the LLBC needs to meet with Democrats before a legislative session begins to set an agenda and line up support where there is agreement. In other words, the LLBC agenda ought to be part of the Democratic Party's agenda.

As the Republicans take power in the legislature, the white Democrats and the LLBC will need to rally around their shared party label if they hope to keep some power in the legislature. We have seen recent signs of a possible unification of the two Democratic factions, as members of the LLBC are now starting to work their way into the party leadership as well. It will be interesting to see whether these factions can possibly work together and protect their political power.

Another route is to initiate more formal alliances with members who share similar district characteristics beyond racial composition, whether they are conservative, liberal, or moderate legislators. The districts represented by LLBC members are poor, as are the districts represented by many white legislators, whether Republican or Democratic. There seems to be no reason why the LLBC and members from such districts cannot form coalitions and formulate policy goals before a legislative session begins. The LLBC is important, but it has failed if it cannot achieve policy success. One way to achieve policy success would be to bring to the table a more diverse group based on policy interests, who could work together to set an agenda based on district similarities and shared problems beyond race. Attempting to diversify coalition partners reflects the call of Marc Morial, a former mayor of New Orleans who also served briefly as a caucus member. Lawmakers, Morial stated, "should work to bridge the racial and class disparities that form a chasm between the haves and the have-nots."[4]

One of the most essential ways to increase success is to end racial prejudice as well as the perception of racial prejudice. Without a doubt this is the most difficult task facing legislators not only in Louisiana but in the entire American system. Many LLBC members attributed their lack of policy success to racial prejudice. Our research has shown that black-interest legislation sponsored by nonblack legislators was more likely to pass than black-interest legislation sponsored by black legislators and that black legislators from New Orleans were least likely to successfully represent their constituents by passing new legislation. We are not suggesting that these findings point directly to racial prejudice, but they do force us to ask why black-interest legislation is more likely to pass when it is sponsored by a white legislator and why black legislators from New Orleans tend to fail in their attempts to pass legislation. A possible answer to the first question might be that white sponsorship of black-interest legislation sends a cue to other white members that the black-interest legislation is acceptable. And a possible answer to the second question

Conclusion

might be that black sponsorship of a bill sends a cue to white members that the legislation specifically targets black constituents. In both cases, some white legislators may simply not support race-specific policies.

We argue that one possible solution is to form biracial coalitions on specific policies and to frame policy issues broadly. In other words, the LLBC should focus on what it does best, and that is communication, but the caucus should also work on communicating not just to their constituents but to the entire state and signal to the rest of the legislature that the LLBC is necessary to finding legislative solutions that benefit everyone in the state and not just racially divided constituencies.

Lastly, a more provocative strategy, we believe, is for black candidates to run independently of the two major parties. In other words, they should form their own political party. Then they would not be beholden to just one of the major parties, but would have the option of working with both the Democrats and the Republicans to achieve their goals. Some might argue that this would only hinder black legislators from bettering the conditions of their constituents. But based on our findings, it is apparent that aligning with the Democrats does not yield much success for the LLBC, since Republicans fare better than black Democrats in getting bills passed. While it is true that black legislators are appointed to committee chairmanships (of committees that do not directly appropriate money) and to the positions of speaker pro tempore or senate president pro tempore (mostly ceremonial positions without real power), these appointments have not yielded much policy success. For example, the committees black legislators chair may pass legislation important to their constituents out of committee, but when those policies get a full vote in the house or the senate, they are more likely to fail. Consequently, these positions, although very important, seem to be aimed at making the leadership and legislators feel good about themselves. With the legislature evenly divided between Democrats and Republicans, a new black political party might play a pivotal role in brokering deals, in essence providing a swing vote. Both parties would need to secure commitments from this new black political party, especially on money bills, which require a two-thirds vote to pass. We believe that the LLBC would be in a much better position to pass some of its priority legislation, especially if Democrats were not willing to work with the LLBC.

In the end, there should be no question about the importance of the LLBC. LLBC members play an important role in passing legislation and in connecting their constituents to the state government. More important, whether or not they succeed in passing legislation, they serve as the legislature's conscience, standing up for the poor and the disenfranchised. Thus, it is our view that the need for the LLBC remains. In the words of Marguerite Ross Barnett, "As long as being black remains a powerful ascriptive category, subject to provocative and emotional politicization, collective action through legislative caucuses remains a plausible strategy."[5]

Appendix
Policy Coding

For the 2005 and 2006 regular and special sessions of the Louisiana legislature, we collected primary-source data on all bills and resolutions introduced. We were able to determine sponsorship, committee information, voting history, and roll-call outcomes from information collected from the Louisiana legislative website. We also collected bill summaries from the website, and we used these summaries to code each piece of legislation for policy areas.

General Policy Coding

To code for policy, we set up a multistage process to ensure accurate results. First we used the coding scheme available at www.indiana.edu/~ral/codes.htm. This scheme is based on the codebook used by Frank Baumgartner and Bryan D. Jones in their Policy Agendas Project[1] and on the description of codes by E. Scott Adler and John Wilkerson in the Congressional Bills Project (www.congressionalbills.org). There are 22 main categories, and each main category is divided into various subcategories. The coders had the option of placing each bill into a primary and a secondary category or into a single general main category if none of the subcategories precisely fit the bill. During the coding process, as an inter-coder reliability check we randomly had multiple coders duplicate their coding to check for coding consistency.

Coding for Black-Interest and Race-Specific Policies

Determining whether legislation dealt with the black community was a key component of our research process. After coding all bills and resolutions for a primary and a secondary policy area, we then determined which bills fit into our categories of general black-interest and race-specific legislation. We relied on previous research by Kathleen Bratton, Kerry Haynie, and Kathleen Gamble in our selection process.[2] As a final check, we read the full-text version of randomly selected bills to make sure that our codes were based on bill summaries that fit the actual content of the bills.

We do not mean to imply that the policy areas we categorize as black-interest areas are the exclusive domain of black legislators, but rather that these specific policy areas often apply directly to issues that face the black community. Poverty, social welfare, community housing, and so forth, are concerns of other constituents as well, but they often play a central role in the everyday lives of many blacks. Our aim was to determine which issues were most closely associated with black interests based on previous research, media reports, and accepted conventional wisdom.

We then determined which policy areas were most directly related to race or most often associated with racial issues and concerns. For this category, we limited our coding to bills dealing directly with affirmative action, civil rights and minority issues, and social welfare.

Below we list the specific policy categories we include under general black-interest legislation:

General minority-group, civil rights issues
- Minority-group discrimination
- Voting rights and issues

Community development and housing
- Housing and community development
- Urban economic development and general urban issues
- Low- and middle-income housing programs and needs
- Housing assistance for homeless and homeless issues
- Secondary mortgage market
- State public housing
- Tenants' rights

Education
- Education of underprivileged students

- Early schooling (Head Start)
- Schools for troubled and high-risk kids
- Schools for pregnant teens
- Equality of facilities
- Admissions
- Student aid
- Tuition and fees
- Funding of schools
- Teacher training and certification
- Discipline
- Student safety
- Free-lunch programs
- Proficiency tests
- Prevention of dropping out
- School facilities

Family
- Marriage
- Divorce
- Domestic abuse
- Child support
- Child protection
- Counseling programs
- Adoption
- Child visitation
- Family employee benefits
- Day care
- Abandonment
- Child custody

Health care
- Health-care reform, costs, and availability
- Medicare and Medicaid
- Infant and child health
- Family health care
- Illegal drug abuse, treatment, and education

- Specific diseases and illnesses
- Drug and alcohol abuse and treatment
- Health coverage

Labor, employment, and immigration
- Employment training
- Employee benefits
- Unemployment benefits
- Youth employment and youth Job Corps programs
- Parental leave and child care
- Affirmative action

Law and crime
- Illegal drug production, trafficking, and control
- Prisons
- Juvenile crime and the juvenile justice system
- Riots and crime prevention
- Death penalty
- Surveillance of crimes
- Sentencing and punishment
- Public-defender system
- Rights of the accused
- Hate crimes

Social welfare
- Food stamps and food assistance
- Poverty and assistance for low-income families
- Elderly issues and elderly-assistance programs
- Assistance to the disabled and handicapped
- Social services

Transportation
- Mass transportation
- Public works

Notes

INTRODUCTION

1. *Cracked* is popular redistricting jargon to describe many districts that surround majority-minority districts. Packing minority voters into districts leads to the surrounding districts' having fewer Democratic voters.

2. See Kerry L. Haynie, *African American Legislators in the American States* (New York: Columbia University Press, 2001); Tyson King-Meadows and Thomas F. Schaller, *Devolution and Black State Legislators: Challenges and Choices in the Twenty-First Century* (Albany: State University of New York Press, 2006); and Robert Singh, *The Congressional Black Caucus: Racial Politics in the U.S. Congress* (Thousand Oaks, CA: Sage, 1998).

3. See Wayne Parent, *Inside the Carnival: Unmasking Louisiana Politics* (Baton Rouge: Louisiana State University Press, 2004).

4. All 32 members of the LLBC are Democrats, and all of the Republicans are white. For previous research using the same breakdown, see Keith E. Hamm, Robert Harmel, and Robert J. Thompson, "Impacts of Districting Change on Voting Cohesion and Representation," *Journal of Politics* 43 (1981): 544–55; Keith E. Hamm, Robert Harmel, and Robert J. Thompson, "Ethnic and Partisan Minorities in Two Southern State Legislatures," *Legislative Studies Quarterly* 8 (1983): 177–89; and Robert Harmel, Keith Hamm, and Robert Thompson, "Black Voting Cohesion and Distinctiveness in Three Southern Legislatures," *Social Science Quarterly* 64 (1983): 183–92.

1. BLACK ELECTORAL POLITICS

1. In one CNN/Opinion Research Corporation poll, 71 percent of African Americans thought there would never be a black president in their lifetime. See CNN, "In Poll, African Americans Say Elections a Dream Come True," www.cnn.com/2008/POLITICS/11/11/obama.poll/index.html.

2. Lawrence J. Hanks, *The Struggle for Black Political Empowerment in Three Georgia Counties* (Knoxville: University of Tennessee Press, 1987).

3. Manning Marable, *Black Leadership* (New York: Columbia University Press, 1998), 3.

4. United States Constitution, Article I, Section 9, Clause 1.

5. George Frederickson, *The Negro as a Beast: Southern Negrophobia at the Turn of the Century* (New York: Harper and Row, 1971).

6. Frederick Douglass, "What to the Slave Is the Fourth of July?" in *Let Nobody Turn Us Around: Voices of Resistance, Reform, and Renewal*, ed. Manning Marable and Leith Mullings (New York: Rowman and Littlefield, 1999), 87.

7. Ibid., 88.

8. Henry Billings Brown, "Majority Opinion in *Plessy v. Ferguson*," in *Desegregation and the Supreme Court*, ed. Benjamin Munn Ziegler (Boston: D. C. Heath, 1958), 50–51.

9. The direct election of senators did not begin until 1913 and the ratification of the Seventeenth Amendment.

10. Hanks, *Struggle for Black Political Empowerment*, 14.

11. Ibid., 25.

12. Charles S. Bullock III and Ronald Keith Gaddie, *The Triumph of Voting Rights in the South* (Norman: University of Oklahoma Press, 2009), 3–4. Bullock and Gaddie provide an extensive discussion of the electoral gains, by state, since the passage of the VRA.

13. See Joint Center for Political and Economic Studies, *Black Elected Officials: A National Roster, 2000* (Washington, DC: Joint Center for Political and Economic Studies Press, 2000). The total number of electoral successes is for all races in 1998 and 1999 from all fifty states, the District of Columbia, and the Virgin Islands.

14. Michael Owens, "Why Blacks Support Vouchers," *New York Times*, 26 February 2002, A27.

15. David Campbell and Joe R. Feagin, "Black Politics in the South: A Descriptive Analysis," *Journal of Politics* 37 (1975): 129–62; Joint Center for Political and Economic Studies, *Black Elected Officials*.

16. Richard Engstrom and Michael McDonald, "The Election of Blacks to City Councils: Clarifying the Impact of Electoral Arrangements on the Seats/Population Relationship," *American Political Science Review* 75 (1981): 344–54.

17. John Kramer, "The Election of Blacks to City Councils: A 1970 Status Report and a Prolegomenon," *Journal of Black Studies* 1 (1971): 443–76.

18. Campbell and Feagin, "Black Politics in the South"; Joint Center for Political and Economic Studies, *Black Elected Officials*.

19. Campbell and Feagin, "Black Politics in the South."

20. Joint Center for Political and Economic Studies, *Black Elected Officials*.

21. David Campbell and Joe Feagin, "Black Electoral Victories in the South," *Phylon* 45 (1984): 331–45.

22. For more detailed information on black governors, see "Emerging from the Shadows, 1775–1819: The Black Governors," www.hartford-hwp.com/HBHP/exhibit/03/1.html.

23. Ibid.

24. Joint Center for Political and Economic Studies, *Black Elected Officials*.

25. Bullock and Gaddie, *Triumph of Voting Rights*.

26. For details on the number of black elected officials from 1947 to 2001, see Joint Center for Political and Economic Studies, *Black Elected Officials;* and Lucius Baker, Mack H. Jones, and Katherine Tate, *African Americans and the American Political System* (Upper Saddle River, NJ: Prentice Hall, 1999).

27. Baker, Jones, and Tate, *African Americans and the American Political System*, 256.

28. See, e.g., UXL Biographies, *Shirley Chisholm* (Detroit: Gale Research and Compton's Encyclopedia, 1996).

29. David Butler and Bruce Cain, *Congressional Redistricting: Comparative and Theoretical Perspectives* (New York: Macmillan, 1992).

30. Baker, Jones, and Tate, *African Americans and the American Political System*, 264.

31. Ibid., 259.

32. Joint Center for Political and Economic Studies, *The Black Vote in 2000* (Washington, DC: Joint Center for Political and Economic Studies Press, 2000).

33. Carol M. Swain, *Black Faces, Black Interests: The Representation of African Americans in Congress* (Cambridge: Cambridge University Press, 1993).

34. Charles L. Prysby, "The 1990 U.S. Senate Election in North Carolina," in *Race, Politics, and Governance in the United States*, ed. Huey L. Perry (Gainesville: University Press of Florida, 1996), 47–61.

35. Marilyn Davis and Alex Willingham, "Andrew Young and the Georgia State Elections of 1990," in *Dilemmas of Black Politics: Issues of Leadership and Strategy*, ed. Georgia Persons (New York: HarperCollins, 1993), 176–92.

36. Ibid., 168–69.

37. Susan T. Fiske, "Stereotyping, Prejudice, and Discrimination," in *The Handbook of Social Psychology*, ed. Daniel Gilbert, Susan T. Fiske, and Gardner Lindzey, 4th ed. (New York: McGraw-Hill, 1998), 361.

38. Gordon Allport, *The Nature of Prejudice* (Reading, MA: Addison-Wesley, 1954), 175–76.

39. Fiske, "Stereotyping, Prejudice, and Discrimination," 362.

40. Shelley E. Taylor, "A Categorization Approach to Stereotyping," in *Cognitive Process in Stereotyping and Intergroup Behavior*, ed. D. L. Hamilton (Hillsdale, NJ: Erlbaum, 1981), 83–114.

41. Shelley E. Taylor et al., "Categorical and Contextual Basis of Person Memory and Stereotyping," *Journal of Personality and Social Psychology* 36 (1975): 778–93.

42. Fiske, "Stereotyping, Prejudice, and Discrimination," 364.

43. David L. Hamilton and Tina K. Trolier, "Stereotypes and Stereotyping: An Overview of the Cognitive Approach," in *Prejudice, Discrimination, and Racism*, ed. John Dovidio and Samuel L. Gaertner (New York: Academic, 1986), 133.

44. Travis L. Dixon, "A Social Cognitive Approach to Studying Racial Stereotyping in the Mass Media," *African American Research Perspectives* 6 (2000): 60–68.

45. "Beyond the News," Third Way Café, www.thirdway.com.

46. Dixon, "Social Cognitive Approach," 60.

47. Jeff Smith, *Tell Me Who I Am: Race Representation at the Movies* (Grand Rapids, MI: Grand Rapids Institute of Democracy, 2003), 1, griid.org/reports/ (last accessed 4 February 2011).

48. Robert M. Entman and Andrew Rojecki, *The Black Image in the White Mind: Media and Race in America* (Chicago: University of Chicago Press, 2000), 83.

49. Kathleen H. Jamieson, *Dirty Politics: Deception, Distraction, and Democracy* (New York: Oxford University Press, 1992).

50. Entman and Rojecki, *Black Image in the White Mind*, 83.

51. "Beyond the News."

52. Ronald Humphrey and Howard Schuman, "The Portrayal of Blacks in Magazine Advertisements, 1950–1982," *Public Opinion Quarterly* 48 (1984): 558.

53. Lawrence Bowen and Jill Schmid, "Minority Presence and Portrayal in Mainstream Magazine Advertising," *Journalism and Mass Communication Quarterly* 74 (1997): 134–46.

54. Christopher Campbell, *Race, Myth, and the News* (Thousand Oaks, CA: Sage, 1995).

55. See Sherryl Graves, "Television, the Portrayal of African-Americans, and the Development of Children's Attitudes," in *Children and Television: Images in a Changing Sociocultural World*, ed. G. L. Berry and J. K. Asamen (Beverly Hills, CA: Sage, 1993), 179–90; Tom Smith, *Ethnic Images*, GSS Topical Report, no. 19 (Chicago: National Opinion Research Center, 1990); and Mark Peffley and Jon Hurwitz, "Public Perceptions of Race and Crime: The Role of Racial Stereotypes," *American Journal of Political Science* 41 (1997): 377.

56. Lee Sigelman and Steven A. Tuch, "Metastereotypes: Blacks' Perceptions of Whites' Stereotypes of Blacks," *Public Opinion Quarterly* 61 (1997): 88.

57. Reynolds Farley et al., "Stereotypes and Segregation: Neighborhoods in the Detroit Area," *American Journal of Sociology* 100 (1994): 753.

58. Jack Citrin, Donald Green, and David O. Sears, "White Reactions to Black Candidates: When Does Race Matter?" *Public Opinion Quarterly* 54 (1990): 74–96.

59. For more information on how policy positions of black candidates affect voting behavior, see David O. Sears, Leonie Huddy, and Lynitta G. Shaffer, "A Schematic Variant of Symbolic Politics Theory: As Applied to Racial and Gender Equality," in *Political Cognition*, ed. Richard Lau and David O. Sears (Hillside, NJ: Erlbaum, 1986); and David O. Sears, Richard Lau, et al., "Self-Interest versus Symbolic Politics in Policy Attitudes and Presidential Voting," *American Political Science Review* 74 (1980): 670–84.

60. Nayda Terkildsen, "When White Voters Evaluate Black Candidates: The Processing Implications of Candidate Skin Color, Prejudice, and Self-Monitoring," *American Journal of Political Science* 37 (1993): 1032–53.

61. David O. Sears, Colette Van Laar, et al., "Is It Really Racism? The Origins of White Americans' Opposition to Race-Targeted Policies," *Public Opinion Quarterly* 61 (1997): 16–53.

62. Carol Sigelman et al., "Black Candidates, White Voters: Understanding Racial Bias in Political Perceptions," *American Journal of Political Science* 39 (1995): 243–65.

63. Murray Edelman, *The Politics of Misinformation* (Cambridge: Cambridge University Press, 2001), 13.

64. Sigelman et al., "Black Candidates, White Voters"; Citrin, Green, and Sears, "White Reactions to Black Candidates."

65. Swain, *Black Faces, Black Interests*, 209.

66. Raphael L Sonenshein, "Can Black Candidates Win Statewide Elections?" *Political Science Quarterly* 105 (1990): 219–41.

67. For more information on the effects of campaign strategy, see Linda F. Williams,

"White/Black Perceptions of the Electability of Black Political Candidates," *National Political Science Review* 2 (1990): 145–64; Huey Perry, "Deracialization as an Analytical Construct in American Urban Politics," *Urban Affairs Quarterly* 27 (1991): 181–91; and Robert C. Smith, "Recent Elections and Black Politics: The Maturation or Death of Black Politics?" *PS: Political Science and Politics* 23 (1990): 160–63.

68. Roger K. Oden, "The Election of Carol Moseley-Braun in the U.S. Senate Race in Illinois," in *Race, Politics, and Governance in the United States,* ed. Huey L. Perry (Gainesville: University Press of Florida, 1996), 47.

69. Ibid.

70. Judson Jeffries, "U.S. Senator Edward W. Brooke and Governor L. Douglas Wilder Tell Political Scientists How Blacks Can Win High-Profile Statewide Office," *PS: Political Science and Politics* 32 (1999): 585–86.

71. Ibid.

72. Alvin Schexnider, "The Politics of Pragmatism: An Analysis of the 1989 Gubernatorial Election in Virginia," *PS: Political Science and Politics* 32 (1999): 155.

73. Ibid., 154.

74. R. Smith, "Recent Elections and Black Politics."

75. William Bianco, *Trust: Representatives and Constituents* (Ann Arbor: University of Michigan Press, 1994), 153.

76. Kathleen A. Bratton and Kerry L. Haynie, "Agenda Setting and Legislative Success in State Legislatures: The Effects of Gender and Race," *Journal of Politics* 61 (1999): 659.

77. Jane Mansbridge, "Should Blacks Represent Blacks and Women Represent Women? A Contingent Yes," *Journal of Politics* 61 (1999): 636.

78. Ibid., 637.

79. Deanna Wrenn, "Lawmakers Call for More Black Representation," *Charleston (WV) Daily Mail,* 20 January 2003.

80. Claudine Gay, "Spirals of Trust? The Effect of Descriptive Representation on the Relationship between Citizens and Their Government," *American Journal of Political Science* 46 (2002): 712–32.

81. Mansbridge, "Should Blacks Represent Blacks," 641.

82. Glen Abeny and John D. Hutcheson, "Race Representation and Trust," *Public Opinion Quarterly* 45 (1981): 91–101.

83. Claudine Gay, "The Impact of Black Congressional Representation on the Behavior of Constituents" (paper presented at the annual meeting of the Midwest Political Science Association, Chicago, 18–20 April 1996).

84. Swain, *Black Faces, Black Interests,* 219.

85. Mack H. Jones, "Black Office-Holding and Political Development in the Rural South," *Review of Black Political Economy* 6 (1976): 375–407.

86. Maraleen, D. Shields, "Racial Gerrymandering: Enfranchisement or Political Apartheid?" (paper presented at the Interdisciplinary Research Conference, Drury University, Springfield, MO, 5–6 February 1999), 4.

87. Mansbridge, "Should Blacks Represent Blacks," 651.

88. Katherine Tate, "The Political Representation of Blacks in Congress: Does Race Matter?" *Legislative Studies Quarterly* 26 (2001): 626.

89. Ibid., 623.

90. Charles Cameron, David Epstein, and Sharyn O'Halloran, "Do Majority-Minority Districts Maximize Substantive Black Representation in Congress?" *American Political Science Review* 90 (1996): 794.

91. Bratton and Haynie, "Agenda Setting and Legislative Success," 659.

92. Mansbridge, "Should Blacks Represent Blacks," 644.

93. Richard F. Fenno Jr., *Home Style: House Members in Their Districts* (Boston: Little, Brown, 1978), 115.

94. Bratton and Haynie, "Agenda Setting and Legislative Success," 667.

95. Ibid., 670.

96. Kathryn Yatrakis, *Electoral Demands and Political Benefits: Minority as Majority; A Case Study of Two Newark Elections, 1970, 1974* (New York: Columbia University Press, 1981).

97. Rufus Browning, Dale Rogers Marshall, and David Tabb, *Protest Is Not Enough: The Struggle of Blacks and Hispanics for Equality in Urban Politics* (Berkeley and Los Angeles: University of California Press, 1984).

98. Swain, *Black Faces, Black Interests*.

99. Mansbridge, "Should Blacks Represent Blacks," 640.

100. Swain, *Black Faces, Black Interests*, 73.

101. David Epstein and Sharyn O'Halloran, "Measuring the Electoral and Policy Impact of Majority-Minority Voting Districts: Candidates of Choice, Equal Opportunity, and Representation," *American Journal of Political Science* 43 (1999): 367–95.

102. Cameron, Epstein, and O'Halloran, "Do Majority-Minority Districts Maximize," 810.

103. Christian R. Grose, *Congress in Black and White: Race and Representation in Washington and at Home* (Cambridge: Cambridge University Press, 2011).

2. AN OVERVIEW OF BLACK CAUCUS HISTORY

1. Eddie Bernice Johnson (D-TX), *Congressional Record*, 21 March 2001.

2. Charles A. Gliozzo, "John Jones and the Black Convention Movement," *Journal of Black Studies* 3 (1972): 227–36.

3. Bella Gross, "The First Negro National Convention," *Journal of Negro History* 31 (1946): 435–43.

4. Richard Allen, "Address to the Free People of Colour of these United States," in *Minutes of the Proceedings of the National Negro Conventions, 1830–1864*, ed. Howard Holman (New York: Arno, 1913), 130.

5. Ibid., 130.

6. Howard H. Bell, "National Negro Conventions of the Middles 1840s: Moral Suasion vs. Political Action," *Journal of Negro History* 42 (1957): 260. We rely on this article for much of the information in the following paragraphs.

7. Ibid., 260.

8. Jane H. Pease and William H. Pease, "Negro Conventions and the Problem of Black Leadership," *Journal of Black Studies* 2 (1971): 40.

9. Robert C. Smith, *We Have No Leaders: African Americans in the Post–Civil Rights Era* (Albany: State University of New York Press, 1996), 39.

10. Ibid., 75–76.

11. Hanes Walton, *Black Political Parties: An Historical and Political Analysis* (New York: Free Press, 1972), 199.

12. Ibid., 200.

13. Willie Legette, "The South Carolina Legislative Black Caucus, 1970 to 1988," in "African American State Legislative Politics," ed. Charles E. Jones, special issue, *Journal of Black Studies* 30 (2000): 839–58.

14. Ibid., 842.

15. Susan Webb Hammond, "Congressional Caucuses and Party Leaders in the House of Representatives," *Political Science Quarterly* 106 (1991): 301–22.

16. Alan Fiellin, "The Function of Informal Groups in the Legislative Institutions," *Journal of Politics* 24 (1962): 76.

17. Burdett A. Loomis, "Congressional Caucuses and the Politics of Representation," in *Congress Reconsidered*, ed. Lawrence C. Dodd and Bruce Oppenheimer (Washington, DC: CQ Press, 1981), 203.

18. Sven Groennings, "The Clubs in Congress: The House Wednesday Group," in *To Be a Congressman: The Promise and the Power*, ed. Sven Groennings and Jonathan P. Hawley (Washington, DC: Acropolis Books, 1973) .

19. Fiellin, "Function of Informal Groups," 78.

20. Roxanne Gile and Charles E. Jones, "Congressional Racial Solidarity: Exploring Congressional Black Caucus Voting Cohesion, 1971–1990," *Journal of Black Studies* 25 (1995): 622.

21. Marcus D. Pohlman, *Black Politics in Conservative America*, 2nd ed. (New York: Longman, 1999).

22. Marguerite Ross Barnett, "The Congressional Black Caucus," *Proceedings of the Academy of Political Science* 32 (1975): 36.

23. U.S. Congress, House, Office of History and Preservation, Office of the Clerk, *Black Americans in Congress, 1870–2007* (Washington, DC: GPO, 2008). See also baic.house.gov/historical-essays/essay.html?intSectionID=46.

24. Barnett, "Congressional Black Caucus," 39.

25. For a good overview of the impact of the Voting Rights Act on black electoral success, see Bullock and Gaddie, *Triumph of Voting Rights*.

26. Michael Clemons and Charles E. Jones, "African American Legislative Politics in Virginia," in "African American State Legislative Politics," ed. Charles E. Jones, special issue, *Journal of Black Studies* 30 (2000): 744–67.

27. Robert Holmes, "The Georgia Legislative Black Caucus," *Journal of Black Studies* 30 (2000): 768–90.

28. Of the states that do not have a caucus, Nevada is the only one with a black Republican legislator.

29. South Carolina Legislative Black Caucus, *By-Laws of the South Carolina Legislative Black Caucus* (Columbia, 1980), 1.

30. Missouri Legislative Black Caucus Foundation, www.mlbcf.com.

31. Charles Vincent, "Negro Legislators in Louisiana during Reconstruction" (PhD diss., Louisiana State University and Agricultural and Mechanical College, 1973), 51, 63. Much of the historical information in this section is based on Vincent's dissertation.

32. *Official Journal of the Proceedings of the Convention for Framing a Constitution for the State of Louisiana* (New Orleans: J. B. Roudanez, 1867–68), 7.

33. Vincent, "Negro Legislators," 51.

34. *Constitution of the State of Louisiana* (New Orleans: Republican Office, 1875), 4–5.

35. Vincent, "Negro Legislators," 72–73.

36. Donald W. Davis, "Ratification of the Constitution of 1868—Records of Votes," *Louisiana History* 6 (1965): 301–5.

37. Vincent, "Negro Legislators," 90.

38. Hanks, *Struggle for Black Political Empowerment*, 17.

39. Richard Bardolph, *The Civil Rights Record* (New York: Thomas J. Crowell, 1970), 62–63.

40. Hanks, *Struggle for Black Political Empowerment*, 17.

41. This list is based on the historical accounts from our interviews as well as information provided at the LLBC's official webpage, www.llbc.louisiana.gov/.

42. Authors' interview with member of the LLBC. Chapter 3 provides more detail on our interviews.

3. VIEWS FROM THE LOUISIANA LEGISLATIVE BLACK CAUCUS

1. See James Button and David Hedge, "Legislative Life in the 1990s: A Comparison of Black and White State Legislators," *Legislative Studies Quarterly* 21 (1996): 199–218; David Hedge, James Button, and Mary Spear, "Accounting for the Quality of Black Legislative Life: The View from the States," *American Journal of Political Science* 40 (1996): 82–98; and David M. Hedge and David B. Conklin, "Black Legislative Life in the American States" (paper presented at the annual State Politics and Policy Conference, Milwaukee, WI, 24–25 May 2002).

2. Button and Hedge, "Legislative Life in the 1990s," 82.

3. Ibid., 93.

4. Parent, *Inside the Carnival*, 2.

5. Ibid., 84. See also Alan Rosenthal, *Engines of Democracy: Politics and Policymaking in State Legislatures* (Washington, DC: CQ Press, 2009).

6. Parent, *Inside the Carnival*, 84.

7. In this chapter we present data up to the 2003 election, that is, before the legislative sessions examined in the later chapters. We note any significant changes in the demographics resulting from the 2007 elections.

8. Ibid.

9. In 2008 Governor Bobby Jindal persuaded the legislature to institute new ethics-reform

laws, in part to curb some of the interest groups' power. See Rosenthal, *Engines of Democracy*, for more information.

10. Randy K. Haynie, *Louisiana Legislature, 2004–2008: Grass Roots Guide* (Baton Rouge, LA: Louisiana Governmental Studies, 2004).

11. Michael Dawson, *Behind the Mule: Race and Class in African-American Politics* (Princeton, NJ: Princeton University Press, 1994); Robert Sellers et al., "Racial Identity, Racial Discrimination, Perceived Stress, and Psychological Distress among African American Young Adults," *Journal of Health and Social Behavior* 44 (2003): 302–17.

12. For more details on the MMRI, see www.lsa.umich.edu/aari/.

13. John C. Wahlke et al., *The Legislative System* (New York: John Wiley, 1962), 8.

14. James B. Johnson and Philip E. Secret, "Focus and Style Representational Roles of Congressional Black and Hispanic Black Caucus Members," *Journal of Black Studies* 26 (1996): 248.

15. Heinz Eulau and Paul D. Karps, "The Puzzle of Representation: Specifying Components of Responsiveness," *Legislative Studies Quarterly* 2 (1977): 233–54.

16. Heinz Eulau et al., "The Role of the Representative: Some Empirical Observations on the Theory of Edmund Burke," *American Political Science Review* 53 (1959): 742–56.

17. Johnson and Secret, "Focus and Style Representational Roles."

18. See ibid.

4. SETTING THE AGENDA

1. Robert Travis Scott, "Black Caucus Presses Agenda; Issues Range beyond Recovery from Storm," *New Orleans Times-Picayune*, 31 March 2006.

2. Bratton and Haynie, "Agenda Setting and Legislative Success."

3. Douglas R. Arnold, *The Logic of Collective Action* (New Haven, CT: Yale University Press, 1990); E. E. Schattschneider, *The Semi-Sovereign People* (New York: Holt, Rinehart, and Winston, 1960).

4. See K. Haynie, *African American Legislators*, for a good review of the influence of race on agenda setting.

5. For examples of the impact of race on the types of legislation introduced, see Byron D'Andra Orey, "Black Legislative Politics in Mississippi," in "African American State Legislative Politics," ed. Charles E. Jones, special issue, *Journal of Black Studies* 30 (2000): 791–814; and Legette, "South Carolina Legislative Black Caucus."

6. Bratton and Haynie, "Agenda Setting and Legislative Success," 667.

7. Katherine Tate, *Black Faces in the Mirror: African Americans and Their Representatives in the U.S. Congress* (Princeton, NJ: Princeton University Press, 2003), 81.

8. For more information on our coding, see the appendix. Also see Bratton and Haynie, "Agenda Setting and Legislative Success"; Katrina L. Gamble, "Black Political Representation: An Examination of Legislative Activity within U.S. House Committees," *Legislative Studies Quarterly* 32 (2007): 421–48; and K. Haynie, *African American Legislators*.

9. The most common count-data models usually use either Poisson or negative-binomial

regression. While the two methods are similar, a Poisson model is preferred when the process producing one event is not correlated with the process underlying another. In this case, we argue that the bill-introduction activity of one member is independent of the bill-introduction activity of another member. Theoretically at least, a Poisson model better captures the bill-introduction process. However, methodologically, a negative-binomial model is preferred when there is overdispersion in the dependent variables, since it allows more confidence in the standard errors. Thus, in the black-interest models we use a negative-binomial model, and we use a Poisson model in the race-specific models because it better fits the distribution of the variable. For more information on these models, see Stata Library, "Analyzing Count Data," www.ats.ucla.edu/stat/stata/library/count.htm (last accessed 31 May 2009); Jered Carr and Richard C. Feiock, "State Annexation 'Constraints' and the Frequency of Municipal Annexation," *Political Research Quarterly* 54 (2001): 459–70; and Gary King, "Statistical Models for Political Science Event Counts: Bias in Conventional Procedures and Evidence for the Exponential Poisson Regression Model," *American Journal of Political Science* 32 (1988): 838–63.

10. See the appendix for more details. K. Haynie, *African American Legislators,* is also a good source for details on this coding method.

11. K. Haynie, *African American Legislators.*

12. See ibid.; and Sue Thomas, *How Women Legislate* (New York: Oxford University Press, 1994).

13. See Jonathan Winburn and Jas M. Sullivan, "The Significance of Race and Geography on Legislative Behavior: Exploring the Agenda in Post-Katrina Louisiana" (paper presented at the annual meeting of the Southern Political Science Association, New Orleans, 2008) for more information.

14. See Holmes, "Georgia Legislative Black Caucus."

15. Both negative-binomial and Poisson models are too unstable to report any meaningful coefficients and standard errors with only 23 individuals across four sessions, or 95 total observations. We ran into the same problem when we ran reduced-form models; nor did bootstrapping techniques totally alleviate our methodological concerns. In both the reduced-form and bootstrapping estimations, the small sample size presumably led to inflated standard-error estimates and resulting Type II errors, or not being able to reject the null hypothesis. In other words, the small sample size did not allow the model to show any statistically significant relationship even if a true relationship existed. For more information, see Robert A. Hart Jr. and David H. Clark, "Revisiting Small Sample Problems in Maximum Likelihood Estimation" (paper presented at the annual meeting of the Midwest Political Science Association, Chicago, 15–17 April 1999).

16. David Kessler and Keith Krehbiel, "Dynamics of Cosponsorship," *American Political Science Review* 90 (1996): 1–12.

17. In the Louisiana legislature as in many other legislatures, the number of cosponsors increases as a bill moves forward and especially once it becomes obvious that the bill will pass. Cosponsorship is an easy form of credit taking and a way for legislators to insulate themselves from outside criticism.

5. TURNING BLACK-INTEREST AGENDAS INTO POLICY

1. Marsha Shuler, "Black Lawmakers Leave House Special Session: Legislators Charge Racism in N.O. Election Bill," *Advocate* (Baton Rouge), 14 February 2006, A1.
2. Mark C. Ellickson, "Pathways to Legislative Success: A Path Analytic Study of the Missouri House of Representatives," *Legislative Studies Quarterly* 17 (1992): 285–302.
3. See Michael K. Moore and Sue Thomas, "Explaining Legislative Success in the U.S. Senate: The Role of the Majority and Minority Parties," *Western Political Quarterly* 44 (1990): 959–70; and William D. Anderson, Janet M. Box-Steffensmeier, and Valeria Sinclair-Chapman, "The Keys to Legislative Success in the U.S. House of Representatives," *Legislative Studies Quarterly* 28 (2003): 357–86.
4. Edward B. Hasecke and Jason D. Mycoff, "Party Loyalty and Legislative Success: Are Loyal Majority Party Members More Successful in the U.S. House of Representatives?" *Political Research Quarterly* 60 (2007): 607–17.
5. See John Hibbing, *Congressional Careers: Contours of Life in the U.S. House of Representatives* (Chapel Hill: University of North Carolina Press, 1991); Moore and Thomas, "Explaining Legislative Success"; and Stephen Frantzich, "Who Makes Our Laws? The Legislative Effectiveness of Members of the U.S. Congress," *Legislative Studies Quarterly* 4 (1979): 409–28.
6. See Hibbing, *Congressional Careers*; and Richard, F. Fenno Jr., *Congressmen in Committees* (Boston: Little, Brown, 1973).
7. See Hibbing, *Congressional Careers*; and Fenno, *Congressmen in Committees*.
8. David Mayhew, *Congress: The Electoral Connection* (New Haven, CT: Yale University Press, 1974).
9. See Bianco, *Trust: Representatives and Constituents*; and Frantzich, "Who Makes Our Laws?"
10. Calvin J. Mouw and Michael B. Mackuen, "The Strategic Agenda in Legislative Politics," *American Political Science Review* 86 (1992): 87–105.
11. Anderson, Box-Steffensmeier, and Sinclair-Chapman, "Keys to Legislative Success," 358.
12. Lani Guinier, *The Tyranny of the Majority* (New York: Free Press, 1994). The book is essentially a republication of her essays and arguments that caused the controversy around her nomination. The book came out after the fact.
13. John W. Kingdon, *Congressmen's Voting Decisions*, 3rd ed. (Ann Arbor: University of Michigan Press, 1989).
14. Bratton and Haynie, "Agenda Setting and Legislative Success."
15. See Michelle A. Saint-German, "Does Their Difference Make a Difference? The Impact of Women on Public Policy in the Arizona Legislature," *Social Science Quarterly* 70 (1989): 956–68; Sue Thomas, "The Impact of Women on State Legislative Politics," *Journal of Politics* 53 (1991): 958–76; and Thomas, *How Women Legislate*.
16. Bratton and Haynie, "Agenda Setting and Legislative Success."
17. Kathleen Bratton, "The Behavior and Success of Latino Legislators: Evidence from

the States," *Social Science Quarterly* 87 (2006): 1136–57; Tatcho Mindiola Jr. and Armando Gutierrez, "Chicanos and the Legislative Process: Reality and Illusion in the Politics of Change," in *Latinos and the Political System*, ed. F. C. Garcia (Notre Dame, IN: University of Notre Dame Press, 1988), 349–62. For the opposite view, see Robert R. Preuhs, "Descriptive Representation, Legislative Leadership, and Direct Democracy: Latino Influence on English Only Laws in the States, 1984–2002," *State Politics and Policy Quarterly* 3 (2005): 203–24.

18. Bratton and Haynie, "Agenda Setting and Legislative Success."

19. Orey, "Black Legislative Politics in Mississippi"; Byron D'Andra Orey et al., "Race *and* Gender Matter: Refining Models of Legislative Policy Making in State Legislatures," *Journal of Women, Politics, and Policy* 28 (2007): 97–119.

20. See Mary Hawkesworth, "Congressional Enactments of Race-Gender: Toward a Theory of Race-Gendered Institutions," *American Political Science Review* 97 (2003): 529–50; Hedge, Button, and Spear, "Accounting for the Quality of Black Legislative Life"; and Tate, "Political Representation of Blacks." See Robert R. Preuhs, "The Conditional Effects of Minority Descriptive Representation: Black Legislators and Policy Influence in the American States," *Journal of Politics* 68 (2006): 585–99, for a differing viewpoint.

21. Whether a bill was vetoed by the governor and not overturned is covered by the second category.

22. We also considered using a multinominal logit model that assumes no ranking for the categories. However, we argue that our coding of the bill process does have an inherent ranking. We ran the results using both models as a check and found similar substantive results. Additionally, we also considered the possibility of a selection model (i.e., the Heckman Probit model) but determined that it was not appropriate, since our coding is not censored. Selection models are most appropriate when some observations are censored from the data because they were not selected or did not undergo some process to become part of the sample (e.g., if someone did not register to vote, then they could not vote). In our case, bills that did not make it out of committee are still part of the data set and not censored from our analysis. Thus, maximum likelihood estimation (MLE) models are more appropriate than selection models.

23. See Bratton and Haynie, "Agenda Setting and Legislative Success"; and Jessica C. Gerrity, Tracy Osborn, and Jeanette Morehouse Mendez, "Women and Representation: A Different View of the District?" *Politics & Gender* 3 (2007): 179–200.

24. Peverill Squire, "Member Career Opportunities and the Internal Organization of Legislatures," *Journal of Politics* 50 (1988): 726–44.

25. Hamm, Harmel, and Thompson, "Ethnic and Partisan Minorities."

26. See Ellickson, "Pathways to Legislative Success."

27. Malcolm E. Jewell and Samuel C. Patterson, *The Legislative Process in the United States*, 4th ed. (New York: Random House, 1966).

28. Given the nonpartisan primary format used in Louisiana and the frequency of elections, this designation is more appropriate than the vote total in the previous general election.

29. We considered using a presidential vote as a normal vote measure, but due to high

levels of multicollinearity with group identification, we turned to registration data. For our purposes here, the use of either measure is appropriate. Collinearity remains a concern when using registration data, but the other important characteristics of this measure outweigh this concern.

30. In this analysis, we include only resolutions that dealt with a specific policy area. We drop the bulk of resolutions that deal with individual recognitions.

31. The house committee did not receive any referrals in the 2005 special session.

32. K. Haynie, *African American Legislators*; King-Meadows and Schaller, *Devolution and Black State Legislators*.

33. Cheryl M. Miller, "Agenda-Setting by State Legislative Black Caucuses: Policy Priorities and Factors of Success," *Policy Studies Review* 9 (1990): 339–54.

6. VOTING COHESION, IDEOLOGY, AND COALITIONS

1. Jan Moller, "Blanco's Spending Proposal Stalls: Without Lifting Cap on Spending, Plans for Budget Surplus Stall," *New Orleans Times-Picayune*, 11 December 2006.

2. Gile and Jones, "Congressional Racial Solidarity."

3. Neil Pinney and George Serra, "The Congressional Black Caucus and Vote Cohesion: Placing the Caucus within House Voting Patterns," *Political Research Quarterly* 52 (1999): 583–608.

4. Pohlman, *Black Politics in Conservative America*; Franklin Mixon and Rand Ressler, "Loyal Political Cartels and Committee Assignments in Congress: Evidence from the Congressional Black Caucus," *Public Choice* 108 (2001): 313–30.

5. Arthur Levy and Susan Stoudinger, "Sources of Voting Cues for the Congressional Black Caucus," *Journal of Black Studies* 7 (1976): 39.

6. Carol M. Swain, "Changing Patterns of African-American Representation in Congress," in *The Atomistic Congress*, ed. Allen D. Hertzke and Ronald M. Peters Jr. (Armonk, NY: M. E. Sharpe, 1992), 107–40.

7. Swain, *Black Faces, Black Interests*; R. Cohen, "New Breed for Black Caucus," *National Journal* 19 (1987): 2432–35.

8. M. Dion Thompson, "Black Caucus Having 'Big Year,'" *Baltimore Sun*, 29 March 2001, 1B.

9. Holmes, " Georgia Legislative Black Caucus"; Orey, "Black Legislative Politics in Mississippi."

10. Holmes, "Georgia Legislative Black Caucus," 787.

11. Ibid., 768–90.

12. In most states, the average roll-call vote is not only not competitive but often unanimous. Since few votes are truly competitive in legislatures throughout the country, we adopt the standard 5 percent threshold. For more details, see Alan Rosenthal, *The Decline of Representative Democracy* (Washington, DC: CQ Press, 1998); and Jennifer Hayes Clark et al., "Representation in U.S. Legislatures: The Acquisition and Analysis of U.S. State Legislative Roll-Call Data," *State Politics and Policy Quarterly* 9 (2009): 356–70.

13. See Stewart Rice, *Quantitative Methods in Politics* (New York: Knopf, 1928).

14. Regression models, not included here, find a positive and significant relationship for partisanship and cohesion and a negative and significant relationship for group size and cohesion. A one-party group with fewer members is more likely to show high levels of cohesion than other types of groups, with partisanship being a more powerful explanatory variable than size.

15. See Parent, *Inside the Carnival*, for a good discussion.

16. Keith T. Poole and Howard Rosenthal, *Congress: A Political-Economic History of Roll Call Voting* (Oxford: Oxford University Press, 1997).

17. See John H. Aldrich and James S. Coleman Battista, "Conditional Party Government in the States," *American Journal of Political Science* 46 (2002): 164–72; and Gerald C. Wright and Brian F. Schaffner, "The Influence of Party: Evidence from the State Legislatures," *American Political Science Review* 96 (2002): 367–79. Notable exceptions are Keith Krehbiel, *Pivotal Politics: A Theory of U.S. Lawmaking* (Chicago: University of Chicago Press, 1998); and Krehbiel, "Party Discipline and Measures of Partisanship," *American Journal of Political Science* 44 (2000): 212–27.

18. Jeffery A. Jenkins, "Examining the Bonding Effects of Party: A Comparative Analysis of Roll-Call Voting in the U.S. and Confederate Houses," *American Journal of Political Science* 43 (1999): 144–65; Jenkins, "Examining the Robustness of Ideological Voting: Evidence from the Confederate House of Representatives," *American Journal of Political Science* 44 (2000): 811–22; Wright and Schaffner, "Influence of Party."

19. See Gerald C. Wright and Jennifer Hayes Clark, "Parties and Stability in Legislative Voting Coalitions in the American States" (paper presented at the annual American Political Science Association Meeting, Washington, DC, 1–4 September 2005); and Gerald C. Wright et al., "Minority Caucuses and Roll Call Voting in the State Legislatures" (paper presented at the annual meeting of the American Political Science Association, Boston, 29 August–1 September 2002).

20. For more details on this procedure, please refer to Wright et al., "Minority Caucuses," and the Voteview website (www.voteview.com/) for more information. Additional information is available at www.indiana.edu/~ral; and Hayes Clark et al. "Representation in U.S. Legislatures."

21. The W-NOMINATE procedure works for one chamber at one point in time. A more dynamic version, DW-NOMINATE, allows for comparisons over time within a chamber but not across chambers. For more details, see Keith Poole's website, www.voteview.com/page2a.htm.

22. For more on the use of the presidential vote as a proxy for district partisanship, see Jonathan Winburn, *The Realities of Redistricting: Following the Rules and Limiting Gerrymandering in State Legislative Redistricting* (Lanham, MD: Lexington Books, 2008).

23. Since the results for the 2005 regular session mirror those of the 2006 regular session, we do not show the 2005 results.

24. Wright and Hayes Clark, "Parties and Stability."

CONCLUSION

1. Robert Travis Scott, "Divisions Widening in Black Caucus: LaFonta May Give Up Reins of Group in June," *New Orleans Times-Picayune*, 1 March 2008.
2. Barnett, "Congressional Black Caucus," 50.
3. Jonathan Tilove, "Rep.-elect Anh 'Joseph' Cao Tries to Crack Black Caucus," *New Orleans Times-Picayune*, 18 December 2008.
4. Michelle Krupa, "Marc Morial Highlights Toll of Racial, Class Disparities," *New Orleans Times-Picayune*, 2 July 2010.
5. Barnett, "Congressional Black Caucus," 49.

APPENDIX

1. See Frank R. Baumgartner and Bryan D. Jones, eds., *Policy Dynamics* (Chicago: University of Chicago Press, 2002).
2. See Bratton and Haynie, "Agenda Setting and Legislative Success"; Gamble, "Black Political Representation"; and K. Haynie, *African American Legislators*.

Selected Bibliography

Abeny, Glen, and John D. Hutcheson. "Race Representation and Trust." *Public Opinion Quarterly* 45 (1981): 91–101.
Aldrich, John H. *Why Parties? The Origin and Transformation of Political Parties in America.* Chicago: University of Chicago Press, 1995.
Aldrich, John H., and James S. Coleman Battista. "Conditional Party Government in the States." *American Journal of Political Science* 46 (2002): 164–72.
Allen, Richard. "Address to the Free People of Colour of these United States." In *Minutes of the Proceedings of the National Negro Conventions, 1830–1864,* ed. Howard Holman. New York: Arno, 1913.
Allport, Gordon. *The Nature of Prejudice.* Reading, MA: Addison-Wesley, 1954.
Anderson, William D., Janet M. Box-Steffensmeier, and Valeria Sinclair-Chapman. "The Keys to Legislative Success in the U.S. House of Representatives." *Legislative Studies Quarterly* 28 (2003): 357–86.
Arnold, R. Douglas. *The Logic of Collective Action.* New Haven, CT: Yale University Press, 1990.
Baker, Lucius, Mack H. Jones, and Katherine Tate. *African Americans and the American Political System.* Upper Saddle River, NJ: Prentice Hall, 1999.
Bardolph, Richard. *The Civil Rights Record.* New York: Thomas J. Crowell, 1970.
Barnett, Marguerite Ross. "The Congressional Black Caucus." *Proceedings of the Academy of Political Science* 32 (1975): 34–50.
Baumgartner, Frank R., and Bryan D. Jones, eds. *Policy Dynamics.* Chicago: University of Chicago Press, 2002.
Bell, Howard H. "National Negro Conventions of the Middle 1840s: Moral Suasion vs. Political Action." *Journal of Negro History* 42 (1957): 247–60.
Bianco, William. *Trust: Representatives and Constituents.* Ann Arbor: University of Michigan Press, 1994.
Bowen, Lawrence, and Jill Schmid. "Minority Presence and Portrayal in Mainstream Magazine Advertising." *Journalism and Mass Communication Quarterly* 74 (1997): 134–46.
Bratton, Kathleen. "The Behavior and Success of Latino Legislators: Evidence from the States." *Social Science Quarterly* 87 (2006): 1136–57.

Bratton, Kathleen A., and Kerry L. Haynie. "Agenda Setting and Legislative Success in State Legislatures: The Effects of Gender and Race." *Journal of Politics* 61 (1999): 658–79.

Bratton, Kathleen A., and Leonard P. Ray. "Descriptive Representation, Policy Outcomes, and Municipal Day-Care Coverage in Norway." *American Journal of Political Science* 46 (2002): 428–37.

Brown, Henry Billings. "Majority Opinion in *Plessy v. Ferguson*." In *Desegregation and the Supreme Court*, ed. Benjamin Munn Ziegler, 50–51. Boston: D. C. Heath, 1958.

Browning, Rufus, Dale Rogers Marshall, and David Tabb. *Protest Is Not Enough: The Struggle of Blacks and Hispanics for Equality in Urban Politics*. Berkeley and Los Angeles: University of California Press, 1984.

Bullock, Charles S., III, and Ronald Keith Gaddie. *The Triumph of Voting Rights in the South*. Norman: University of Oklahoma Press, 2009.

Button, James, and David Hedge. "Legislative Life in the 1990s: A Comparison of Black and White State Legislators." *Legislative Studies Quarterly* 21 (1996): 199–218.

Cameron, Charles, David Epstein, and Sharyn O'Halloran. "Do Majority-Minority Districts Maximize Substantive Black Representation in Congress?" *American Political Science Review* 90 (1996): 794–812.

Campbell, Christopher. *Race, Myth, and the News*. Thousand Oaks, CA: Sage, 1995.

Campbell, David, and Joe R. Feagin. "Black Electoral Victories in the South." *Phylon* 45 (1984): 331–45.

———. "Black Politics in the South: A Descriptive Analysis." *Journal of Politics* 37 (1975): 129–62.

Carr, Jered, and Richard C. Feiock. "State Annexation 'Constraints' and the Frequency of Municipal Annexation." *Political Research Quarterly* 54 (2001): 459–70.

Citrin, Jack, Donald Green, and David O. Sears. "White Reactions to Black Candidates: When Does Race Matter?" *Public Opinion Quarterly* 54 (1990): 74–96.

Clark, Jennifer Hayes, Tracy Osborn, Jonathan Winburn, and Gerald Wright. "Representation in U.S. Legislatures: The Acquisition and Analysis of U.S. State Legislative Roll-Call Data." *State Politics and Policy Quarterly* 9 (2009): 356–70.

Clemons, Michael, and Charles E. Jones. "African American Legislative Politics in Virginia." In "African American State Legislative Politics," ed. Charles E. Jones. Special issue, *Journal of Black Studies* 30 (2000): 744–67.

Davidson, R. H., and W. J. Oleszek. *Congress and Its Members*. Washington, DC: CQ Press, 1990.

Davis, Donald W. "Ratification of the Constitution of 1868—Records of Votes." *Louisiana History* 6 (1965): 301–5.

Davis, Marilyn, and Alex Willingham. "Andrew Young and the Georgia State Elections of 1990." In *Dilemmas of Black Politics: Issues of Leadership and Strategy*, ed. Georgia Persons, 176–92. New York: HarperCollins, 1993.

Dawson, Michael. *Behind the Mule: Race and Class in African-American Politics.* Princeton, NJ: Princeton University Press, 1994.

———. *Black Vision: The Roots of Contemporary African-American Political Ideologies.* Chicago: University of Chicago Press, 2001.

Delany, Martin R. "The Condition, Elevation, Emigration, and Destiny of the Colored People of the United States." In *African American Philosophy: Selected Readings,* ed. Tommy L. Lott, 46–65. Upper Saddle River, NJ: Pearson Education, 2002.

Dixon, Travis L. "A Social Cognitive Approach to Studying Racial Stereotyping in the Mass Media." *African American Research Perspectives* 6 (2000): 60–68.

Douglass, Frederick. "An Address to the Colored People of the United States." In *African American Philosophy: Selected Readings,* ed. Tommy L. Lott, 104–7. Upper Saddle River, NJ: Pearson Education, 2002.

———. "The Present and Future of the Colored Race in America." In *African American Philosophy: Selected Readings,* ed. Tommy L. Lott, 107–15. Upper Saddle River, NJ: Pearson Education, 2002.

———. "What to the Slave Is the Fourth of July?" In *Let Nobody Turn Us Around: Voices of Resistance, Reform, and Renewal,* ed. Manning Marable and Leith Mullings, 87–91. New York: Rowman and Littlefield, 1999.

Edelman, Murray. *The Politics of Misinformation.* Cambridge: Cambridge University Press, 2001.

Ellickson, Mark C. "Pathways to Legislative Success: A Path Analytic Study of the Missouri House of Representatives." *Legislative Studies Quarterly* 17 (1992): 285–302.

Engstrom, Richard, and Michael McDonald. "The Election of Blacks to City Councils: Clarifying the Impact of Electoral Arrangements on the Seats/Population Relationship." *American Political Science Review* 75 (1981): 344–54.

Entman, Robert M., and Andrew Rojecki. *The Black Image in the White Mind: Media and Race in America.* Chicago: University of Chicago Press, 2000.

Eulau, Heinz, and Paul D. Karps. "The Puzzle of Representation: Specifying Components of Responsiveness." *Legislative Studies Quarterly* 2 (1977): 233–54.

Eulau, Heinz, John C. Wahlke, William Buchanan, and Leroy C. Ferguson. "The Role of the Representative: Some Empirical Observations on the Theory of Edmund Burke." *American Political Science Review* 53 (1959): 742–56.

Farley, Reynolds, Charlotte Steeh, Maria Krysan, Tara Jackson, and Keith Reeves. "Stereotypes and Segregation: Neighborhoods in the Detroit Area." *American Journal of Sociology* 100 (1994): 750–80.

Fenno, Richard F., Jr. *Congressmen in Committees.* Boston: Little, Brown, 1973.

———. *Home Style: House Members in Their Districts.* Boston: Little, Brown, 1978.

Fiellin, Alan. "The Function of Informal Groups in the Legislative Institutions." *Journal of Politics* 24 (1962): 72–91.

Fiske, Susan T. "Stereotyping, Prejudice, and Discrimination." In *The Handbook of Social*

Psychology, ed. Daniel Gilbert, Susan T. Fiske, and Gardner Lindzey, 357–411. 4th ed. New York: McGraw-Hill, 1998.

Frantzich, Stephen. "Who Makes Our Laws? The Legislative Effectiveness of Members of the U.S. Congress." *Legislative Studies Quarterly* 4 (1979): 409–28.

Frederickson, George. *The Negro as a Beast: Southern Negrophobia at the Turn of the Century.* New York: Harper and Row, 1971.

Gamble, Katrina L. "Black Political Representation: An Examination of Legislative Activity within U.S. House Committees." *Legislative Studies Quarterly* 32 (2007): 421–48.

Garnet, Henry Highland. "An Address to the Slaves of the United States." In *African American Philosophy: Selected Readings,* ed. Tommy L. Lott, 22–27. Upper Saddle River, NJ: Pearson Education, 2002.

Gay, Claudine. "The Impact of Black Congressional Representation on the Behavior of Constituents." Paper presented at the annual meeting of the Midwest Political Science Association, Chicago, 18–20 April 1996.

———. "Spirals of Trust? The Effect of Descriptive Representation on the Relationship between Citizens and Their Government." *American Journal of Political Science* 46 (2002): 712–32.

Gerrity, Jessica C., Tracy Osborn, and Jeanette Morehouse Mendez. "Women and Representation: A Different View of the District?" *Politics & Gender* 3 (2007): 179–200.

Gile, Roxanne, and Charles E. Jones. "Congressional Racial Solidarity: Exploring Congressional Black Caucus Voting Cohesion, 1971–1990." *Journal of Black Studies* 25 (1995): 622–41.

Gliozzo, Charles A. "John Jones and the Black Convention Movement." *Journal of Black Studies* 3 (1972): 227–36.

Graves, Sherryl. "Television, the Portrayal of African-Americans, and the Development of Children's Attitudes." In *Children and Television: Images in a Changing Sociocultural World,* ed. G. L. Berry and J. K. Asamen, 179–90. Beverly Hills, CA: Sage, 1993.

Groennings, Sven. "The Clubs in Congress: The House Wednesday Group." In *To Be a Congressman: The Promise and the Power,* ed. Sven Groennings and Jonathan P. Hawley. Washington, DC: Acropolis Books, 1973.

Grose, Christian R. *Congress in Black and White: Race and Representation in Washington and at Home.* Cambridge: Cambridge University Press, 2011.

Gross, Bella. "The First Negro National Convention." *Journal of Negro History* 31 (1946): 435–43.

Gross, Donald. "Representative Style and Legislative Behavior." *Western Political Quarterly* 31 (1978): 359–71.

Guinier, Lani. *The Tyranny of the Majority.* New York: Free Press, 1994.

Selected Bibliography

Hamilton, David L., and Tina K. Trolier. "Stereotypes and Stereotyping: An Overview of the Cognitive Approach." In *Prejudice, Discrimination, and Racism,* ed. John Dovidio and Samuel L. Gaertner, 127–63. New York: Academic, 1986.

Hamm, Keith E., Robert Harmel, and Robert J. Thompson. "Ethnic and Partisan Minorities in Two Southern State Legislatures." *Legislative Studies Quarterly* 8 (1983): 177–89.

———. "Impacts of Districting Change on Voting Cohesion and Representation." *Journal of Politics* 43 (1981): 544–55.

Hammond, Susan Webb. "Congressional Caucuses and Party Leaders in the House of Representatives." *Political Science Quarterly* 106 (1991): 301–22.

Hanks, Lawrence J. *The Struggle for Black Political Empowerment in Three Georgia Counties.* Knoxville: University of Tennessee Press, 1987.

Harmel, Robert, Keith Hamm, and Robert Thompson. "Black Voting Cohesion and Distinctiveness in Three Southern Legislatures." *Social Science Quarterly* 64 (1983): 183–92.

Hart, Robert A., Jr., and David Clark. "Revisiting Small Sample Problems in Maximum Likelihood Estimation." Paper presented at the annual meeting of the Midwest Political Science Association, Chicago, 15–17 April 1999.

Hasecke, Edward B., and Jason D. Mycoff. "Party Loyalty and Legislative Success: Are Loyal Majority Party Members More Successful in the U.S. House of Representatives?" *Political Research Quarterly* 60 (2007): 607–17.

Hawkesworth, Mary. "Congressional Enactments of Race-Gender: Toward a Theory of Race-Gendered Institutions." *American Political Science Review* 97 (2003): 529–50.

Haynie, Kerry L. *African American Legislators in the American States.* New York: Columbia University Press, 2001.

Haynie, Randy K. *Louisiana Legislature, 2004–2008: Grass Roots Guide.* Baton Rouge: Louisiana Governmental Studies, 2004.

Hedge, David, James Button, and Mary Spear. "Accounting for the Quality of Black Legislative Life: The View from the States." *American Journal of Political Science* 40 (1996): 82–98.

Hedge, David M., and David B. Conklin. "Black Legislative Life in the American States." Paper presented at the annual State Politics and Policy Conference, Milwaukee, WI, 24–25 May 2002.

Hibbing, John. *Congressional Careers: Contours of Life in the U.S. House of Representatives.* Chapel Hill: University of North Carolina Press, 1991.

Holmes, Robert. "The Georgia Legislative Black Caucus." In "African American State Legislative Politics," ed. Charles E. Jones. Special issue, *Journal of Black Studies* 30 (2000): 768–90.

Humphrey, Ronald, and Howard Schuman. "The Portrayal of Blacks in Magazine Advertisements, 1950–1982." *Public Opinion Quarterly* 48 (1984): 551–63.

Jamieson, Kathleen H. *Dirty Politics: Deception, Distraction, and Democracy.* New York: Oxford University Press, 1992.

Jeffries, Judson. "U.S. Senator Edward W. Brooke and Governor L. Douglas Wilder Tell Political Scientists How Blacks Can Win High-Profile Statewide Office." *PS: Political Science and Politics* 32 (1999): 583–87.

Jenkins, Jeffery A. "Examining the Bonding Effects of Party: A Comparative Analysis of Roll-Call Voting in the U.S. and Confederate Houses." *American Journal of Political Science* 43 (1999): 144–65.

———. "Examining the Robustness of Ideological Voting: Evidence from the Confederate House of Representatives." *American Journal of Political Science* 44 (2000): 811–22.

Jewell, Malcolm E. *Representation in State Legislatures.* Lexington: University of Kentucky Press, 1982.

Jewell, Malcolm E., and Samuel C. Patterson. *The Legislative Process in the United States.* 4th ed. New York: Random House, 1966.

Johnson, James B., and Philip E. Secret. "Focus and Style Representational Roles of Congressional Black and Hispanic Black Caucus Members." *Journal of Black Studies* 26 (1996): 245–73.

Joint Center for Political and Economic Studies. *Black Elected Officials: A National Roster, 2000.* Washington, DC: Joint Center for Political and Economic Studies Press, 2000.

———. *The Black Vote in 2000.* Washington, DC: Joint Center for Political and Economic Studies Press, 2000.

Jones, Charles E., and Michael Clemons. "A Model of Racial Crossover Voting: An Assessment of the Wilder Victory." In *Dilemmas of Black Politics: Issues of Leadership and Strategy,* ed. Georgia Persons, 128–46. New York: HarperCollins, 1993.

Jones, Mack H. "Black Mayoral Leadership in Atlanta: A Comment." *National Political Science Review* 2 (1990): 138–44.

———. "Black Office-Holding and Political Development in the Rural South." *Review of Black Political Economy* 6 (1976): 375–407.

Kessler, David, and Keith Krehbiel. "Dynamics of Cosponsorship." *American Political Science Review* 90 (1996): 1–12.

Kinder, Donald R., and David O. Sears. "Prejudice and Politics: Symbolic Racism versus Racial Threats to the Good Life." *Journal of Personality and Social Psychology* 40 (1981): 414–31.

Kinder, Donald, and Nicholas Winter. "Exploring the Racial Divide: Blacks, Whites, and Opinion on National Policy." *American Journal of Political Science* 45 (2001): 439–56.

King, Gary. "Statistical Models for Political Science Event Counts: Bias in Conventional Procedures and Evidence for the Exponential Poisson Regression Model." *American Journal of Political Science* 32 (1988): 838–63.

Selected Bibliography

Kingdon, John W. *Congressmen's Voting Decisions.* 3rd ed. Ann Arbor: University of Michigan Press, 1989.

King-Meadows, Tyson, and Thomas F. Schaller. *Devolution and Black State Legislators: Challenges and Choices in the Twenty-First Century.* Albany: State University of New York Press, 2006.

Kramer, John. "The Election of Blacks to City Councils: A 1970 Status Report and a Prolegomenon." *Journal of Black Studies* 1 (1971): 443–76.

Krehbiel, Keith. "Party Discipline and Measures of Partisanship." *American Journal of Political Science* 44 (2000): 212–27.

———. *Pivotal Politics: A Theory of U.S. Lawmaking.* Chicago: University of Chicago Press, 1998.

Legette, Willie. "The South Carolina Legislative Black Caucus, 1970 to 1988." In "African American State Legislative Politics," ed. Charles E. Jones. Special issue, *Journal of Black Studies* 30 (2000): 839–58.

Levy, Arthur, and Susan Stoudinger. "Sources of Voting Cues for the Congressional Black Caucus." *Journal of Black Studies* 7 (1976): 29–46.

Lilley, W., L. J. Defranco, and W. M. Diefenderfer. *The Almanac of State Legislatures.* Washington, DC: CQ Press, 1994.

Loomis, Burdett A. "Congressional Caucuses and the Politics of Representation." In *Congress Reconsidered,* ed. Lawrence C. Dodd and Bruce Oppenheimer, 204–20. Washington, DC: CQ Press, 1981.

Mansbridge, Jane. "Should Blacks Represent Blacks and Women Represent Women? A Contingent Yes." *Journal of Politics* 61 (1999): 628–57.

Marable, Manning. *Black Leadership.* New York: Columbia University Press, 1998.

Mayhew, David. *Congress: The Electoral Connection.* New Haven, CT: Yale University Press, 1974.

Miller, Cheryl M. "Agenda-Setting by State Legislative Black Caucuses: Policy Priorities and Factors of Success." *Policy Studies Review* 9 (1990): 339–54.

Mindiola, Tatcho, Jr., and Armando Gutierrez. "Chicanos and the Legislative Process: Reality and Illusion in the Politics of Change." In *Latinos and the Political System,* ed. F. C. Garcia, 349–62. Notre Dame, IN: University of Notre Dame Press, 1988.

Mixon, Franklin, and Rand Ressler. "Loyal Political Cartels and Committee Assignments in Congress: Evidence from the Congressional Black Caucus." *Public Choice* 108 (2001): 313–30.

Moore, Michael K., and Sue Thomas. "Explaining Legislative Success in the U.S. Senate: The Role of the Majority and Minority Parties." *Western Political Quarterly* 44 (1990): 959–70.

Mouw, Calvin J., and Michael B. Mackuen. "The Strategic Agenda in Legislative Politics." *American Political Science Review* 86 (1992): 87–105.

Oden, Roger K. "The Election of Carol Moseley-Braun in the U.S. Senate Race in Illinois." In *Race, Politics, and Governance in the United States,* ed. Huey L. Perry, 47–61. Gainesville: University Press of Florida, 1996.

Official Journal of the Proceedings of the Convention for Framing a Constitution for the State of Louisiana. New Orleans: J. B. Roudanez, 1867–68.

Olsen, Marvin. "Social and Political Participation of Blacks." *American Sociological Review* 35 (1970): 682–96.

Orey, Byron D'Andra. "Black Legislative Politics in Mississippi." In "African American State Legislative Politics," ed. Charles E. Jones. Special issue, *Journal of Black Studies* 30 (2000): 791–814.

Orey, Byron D'Andra, Wendy Smooth, Kimberly S. Adams, and Kisha Harris-Clark. "Race and Gender Matter: Refining Models of Legislative Policy Making in State Legislatures." *Journal of Women, Politics, and Policy* 28 (2007): 97–119.

Parent, Wayne. *Inside the Carnival: Unmasking Louisiana Politics.* Baton Rouge: Louisiana State University Press, 2004.

Pease, Jane H., and William H. Pease. "Negro Conventions and the Problem of Black Leadership." *Journal of Black Studies* 2 (1971): 29–44.

Peffley, Mark, and Jon Hurwitz. "Public Perceptions of Race and Crime: The Role of Racial Stereotypes." *American Journal of Political Science* 41 (1997): 375–401.

Perry, Huey. "Black Political and Mayoral Leadership in Birmingham and New Orleans." *National Political Science Review* 2 (1990): 129–95.

———. "Deracialization as an Analytical Construct in American Urban Politics." *Urban Affairs Quarterly* 27 (1991): 181–91.

Persons, Georgia A., and Lenneal J. Henderson. "Mayor of the Colony: Effective Mayoral Leadership as a Matter of Public Perception." *National Political Science Review* 2 (1990): 145–53.

Pinney, Neil, and George Serra. "The Congressional Black Caucus and Vote Cohesion: Placing the Caucus within House Voting Patterns." *Political Research Quarterly* 52 (1999): 583–608.

Pohlman, Marcus D. *Black Politics in Conservative America.* 2nd ed. New York: Longman, 1999.

Poole, Keith T., and Howard Rosenthal. *Congress: A Political-Economic History of Roll Call Voting.* Oxford: Oxford University Press, 1997.

Preston, Michael B. "Symposium: Big City Black Mayors; Have They Made a Difference?" *National Political Science Review* 2 (1990): 129–95.

Preuhs, Robert R. "The Conditional Effects of Minority Descriptive Representation: Black Legislators and Policy Influence in the American States." *Journal of Politics* 68: (2006): 585–99.

———. "Descriptive Representation, Legislative Leadership, and Direct Democracy:

Selected Bibliography

Latino Influence on English Only Laws in the States, 1984–2002." *State Politics and Policy Quarterly* 3 (2005): 203–24.

Prysby, Charles L. "The 1990 U.S. Senate Election in North Carolina." In *Race, Politics, and Governance in the United States*, ed. Huey L. Perry, 47–61. Gainesville: University Press of Florida, 1996.

Rice, Stewart. *Quantitative Methods in Politics*. New York: Knopf, 1928.

Rohde, David W. *Parties and Leaders in the Postreform House*. Chicago: University of Chicago Press, 1991.

Rosenthal, Alan. *The Decline of Representative Democracy*. Washington, DC: CQ Press, 1998.

———. *Engines of Democracy: Politics and Policymaking in State Legislatures*. Washington, DC: CQ Press, 2009.

Saint-German, Michelle A. "Does Their Difference Make a Difference? The Impact of Women on Public Policy in the Arizona Legislature." *Social Science Quarterly* 70 (1989): 956–68.

Schattschneider, E. E. *The Semi-Sovereign People*. New York: Holt, Rinehart, and Winston, 1960.

Schexnider, Alvin. "The Politics of Pragmatism: An Analysis of the 1989 Gubernatorial Election in Virginia." *PS: Political Science and Politics* 23 (1990): 154–56.

Sears, David O., Leonie Huddy, and Lynitta G. Shaffer. "A Schematic Variant of Symbolic Politics Theory: As Applied to Racial and Gender Equality." In *Political Cognition*, ed. Richard Lau and David O. Sears. Hillside, NJ: Erlbaum, 1986.

Sears, David O., Richard Lau, Tom Tyler, and Harris Allen Jr. "Self-Interest versus Symbolic Politics in Policy Attitudes and Presidential Voting." *American Political Science Review* 74 (1980): 670–84.

Sears, David O., Colette Van Laar, Mary Carillo, and Rick Kosterman. "Is It Really Racism? The Origins of White Americans' Opposition to Race-Targeted Policies." *Public Opinion Quarterly* 61 (1997): 16–53.

Sellers, Robert, Cleopatra Caldwell, Karen Schmeelk-Cone, and Marc Zimmerman. "Racial Identity, Racial Discrimination, Perceived Stress, and Psychological Distress among African American Young Adults." *Journal of Health and Social Behavior* 44 (2003): 302–17.

Sellers, R. M., M. A. Smith, J. N. Shelton, A. J. Rowley, and T. M. Chavous. "Multidimensional Model of Racial Identity: A Reconceptualization of African-American Racial Identity." *Personality and Social Psychology Review* 2 (1998): 18–39.

Shields, Maraleen, D. "Racial Gerrymandering: Enfranchisement or Political Apartheid?" Paper presented at the Interdisciplinary Research Conference, Drury University, Springfield, MO, 5–6 February 1999.

Sigelman, Carol, Lee Sigelman, Barbara J. Walkosz, and Michael Nitz. "Black Candidates,

White Voters: Understanding Racial Bias in Political Perceptions." *American Journal of Political Science* 39 (1995): 243–65.

Sigelman, Lee, and Steven A. Tuch. "Metastereotypes: Blacks' Perceptions of Whites' Stereotypes of Blacks." *Public Opinion Quarterly* 61 (1997): 87–101.

Singh, Robert. *The Congressional Black Caucus: Racial Politics in the U.S. Congress.* Thousand Oaks, CA: Sage, 1998.

Smith, Jeff. *Tell Me Who I Am: Race Representation at the Movies.* Grand Rapids, MI: Grand Rapids Institute of Democracy, 2003. griid.org/reports/ (last accessed 4 February 2011).

Smith, Robert C. "Recent Elections and Black Politics: The Maturation or Death of Black Politics?" *PS: Political Science and Politics* 23 (1990): 160–63.

———. *We Have No Leaders: African Americans in the Post–Civil Rights Era.* Albany: State University of New York Press, 1996.

Smith, Tom. *Ethnic Images.* GSS Topical Report, no. 19. Chicago: National Opinion Research Center, 1990.

Sonenshein, Raphael L. "Can Black Candidates Win Statewide Elections?" *Political Science Quarterly* 105 (1990): 219–41.

South Carolina Legislative Black Caucus. *By-Laws of the South Carolina Legislative Black Caucus.* Columbia, SC, 1980.

Squire, Peverill. "Member Career Opportunities and the Internal Organization of Legislatures." *Journal of Politics* 50 (1988): 726–44.

Stone, Chuck. *Black Political Power in America.* New York: Bobbs-Merrill, 1968.

Sullivan, Brenda. "Even at the Turning of the Tide: An Analysis of the North Carolina Legislative Black Caucus." In "African American State Legislative Politics," ed. Charles E. Jones. Special issue, *Journal of Black Studies* 30 (2000): 815–38.

Summers, Mary, and Philip Klinkner. 1990. "The Election of John Daniels as Mayor of New Haven." *PS: Political Science and Politics:* 23: (1990): 141–61.

Swain, Carol M. *Black Faces, Black Interests: The Representation of African Americans in Congress.* Cambridge: Cambridge University Press, 1993.

———. "Changing Patterns of African-American Representation in Congress." In *The Atomistic Congress,* ed. Allen D. Hertzke and Ronald M. Peters Jr., 107–40. Armonk, NY: M. E. Sharpe, 1992.

———. "The Congressional Black Caucus in the Republican Era." Paper prepared for the Congress Project Seminar on Minority Group Leadership in Congress, Woodrow Wilson International Center for Scholars, Washington, DC, 31 January 2003.

Tate, Katherine. *Black Faces in the Mirror: African Americans and Their Representatives in the U.S. Congress.* Princeton, NJ: Princeton University Press, 2003.

———. *From Protest to Politics: The New Black Voters in American Elections.* Cambridge, MA: Harvard University Press, 1993.

———. "The Political Representation of Blacks in Congress: Does Race Matter?" *Legislative Studies Quarterly* 26 (2001): 623–38.

Taylor, Shelley E. "A Categorization Approach to Stereotyping." In *Cognitive Process in Stereotyping and Intergroup Behavior*, ed. D. L. Hamilton, 83–114. Hillsdale, NJ: Erlbaum, 1981.

Taylor, Shelley E., Susan T. Fiske, Nancy L. Etcoff, and Audrey J. Ruderman. "Categorical and Contextual Basis of Person Memory and Stereotyping." *Journal of Personality and Social Psychology* 36 (1975): 778–93.

Terkildsen, Nayda. "When White Voters Evaluate Black Candidates: The Processing Implications of Candidate Skin Color, Prejudice, and Self-Monitoring." *American Journal of Political Science* 37 (1993): 1032–53.

Thomas, Sue. *How Women Legislate*. New York: Oxford University Press, 1994.

———. "The Impact of Women on State Legislative Politics." *Journal of Politics* 53 (1991): 958–76.

Tryman, Mfanya D. "Black Mayoralty: Running the 'Race.'" *Phylon* 35 (1974): 346–58.

Verba, Sidney, and Norman Nie. *Participation in America: Political Democracy and Social Equality*. New York: Harper and Row, 1972.

Vincent, Charles. "Negro Legislators in Louisiana during Reconstruction." PhD diss., Louisiana State University and Agricultural and Mechanical College, 1973.

Wahlke, John C., Heinz Eulau, William Buchanan, and LeRoy Ferguson. *The Legislative System*. New York: John Wiley, 1962.

Walton, Hanes. *Black Political Parties: An Historical and Political Analysis*. New York: Free Press, 1972.

Watson, Sharon. "The Second Time Around: A Profile of Black Mayoral Reelection Campaigns." *Phylon* 45 (1984): 165–78.

Williams, Linda F. "White/Black Perceptions of the Electability of Black Political Candidates." *National Political Science Review* 2 (1990): 145–64.

Wilson, William Julius. *The Truly Disadvantaged: The Inner City, the Underclass, and Public Policy*. Chicago: University of Chicago Press, 1987.

Winburn, Jonathan. *The Realities of Redistricting: Following the Rules and Limiting Gerrymandering in State Legislative Redistricting*. Lanham, MD: Lexington Books, 2008.

Winburn, Jonathan, and Jas M. Sullivan. "The Significance of Race and Geography on Legislative Behavior: Exploring the Agenda in Post-Katrina Louisiana." Paper presented at the annual meeting of the Southern Political Science Association, New Orleans, 9–12 January 2008.

Winn, Mylon. "The Election of Norman Rice as Mayor of Seattle." *PS: Political Science and Politics* 23 (1990): 158–59.

Wright, Gerald C., and Jennifer Hayes Clark. "Parties and Stability in Legislative Voting

Coalitions in the American States." Paper presented at the annual meeting of the American Political Science Association, Washington, DC, 1–4 September 2005.

Wright, Gerald C., Tracy Osborn, Jonathan Winburn, and Jas M. Sullivan. "Minority Caucuses and Roll Call Voting in the State Legislatures." Paper presented at the annual meeting of the American Political Science Association, Boston, 29 August–1 September 2002.

Wright, Gerald C., and Brian F. Schaffner. "The Influence of Party: Evidence from the State Legislatures." *American Political Science Review* 96 (2002): 367–79.

Yatrakis, Kathryn. *Electoral Demands and Political Benefits: Minority as Majority; A Case Study of Two Newark Elections, 1970, 1974*. New York: Columbia University Press, 1981.

Index

Acadiana: average cohesion in, 113
Adler, E. Scott, 141
African American Legislators (Haynie), 78
Africans: arrival in United States, 7–8; voting rights of, 8
agendas: for Louisiana Legislative Black Caucus, 2006, 105–106; turning into policy, 88–108
Alabama: black elected officials in, 11; former slaves in, 9
Alexander, Avery, 42
Allen, Richard, 30
Allport, Gordon, 16
Antoine, C. C., 41
appropriations committees, 51
Arafat, Yasser, 23
Arizona: former slaves in, 9
Arkansas: black elected officials in, 11
Article 13, 40

Bajoie, Diana, 42
Baptists: as black legislators, 50
Barnett, Marguerite Ross, 139
Barthelemy, Sidney John, 42
Baumgartner, Frank, 141
Baylor, Ernest, 51
Behind the Mule (Dawson), 55
Black Codes, 9
black conventions: emergence of, 30
black elected officials: interaction with constituents, 26–27
Black Faces, Black Interests (Swain), 20
black leaders: ideology of, 52–53; income of, 52–53; racial identity of, 53; views on policy, 52–53
black legislation: bill passage and, 91–102; likelihood of passing, 95–102; passage rates of, 92; success in, 89–91
black national parties, 33–34
black nationalism, 32
black state parties, 34
Black Vision (Dawson), 55
black-interest legislation: Louisiana Legislative Black Caucus and, 77–87
blacks: as athletes and musicians, 18–19; as city council members, 11–12; as elected officials, 9; ghettoized, 18; as mayors, 11–12; caucus history of, 29–44; electoral failure and, 20–21; government service of, 10–14; limits of electoral success, 14–16; loyalty to incumbents, 26; portrayal of females, 18; skin as taboo, 18–19; stereotypes of, 17–18; television depiction of, 17–18; voter registration of, 10
Blanco, Kathleen, 70, 109
Bond, Julian, 32
Bradley, Tom, 19, 21
Bratton, Kathleen, 26, 71, 91, 142
Braun, Carol Moseley, 13
Brooke, Edward, 13, 21
Broome, Sharon, 51
Brown, Henry, 9
Brown, Willie, 32
Browning, Rufus, 26
Bruce, Blanche Kelso, 10
Buck: stereotype of, 18
Bush, George, 22
Button, James, 45, 46

Cameron, Charles, 27
Cao, Anh "Joseph," 136
Carter, Karen, 51

categorization, 16–17
Catholics: as black legislators, 50
Caucus: average cohesion of, 113; defined, 35
Charbonnet, Louis, III, 42
Chavous, Tabbye, 54
Chisholm, Shirley, 13
civil rights: early twentieth century and, 10
Civil Rights Act of 1866, 9–10
Civil Rights Act of 1875, 10, 41
Civil Rights Act of 1965, 13
Coalitions, in voting, 121–28
Committee on Militia, 40
Committee on Public Education, 40
Committee on Rules and Regulations, 40
Committee to Draft a Bill of Rights, 40
committees: bills dying in, 104; black service on, 105
Compromise of 1877, 10
Congressional Black Caucus (CBC), 29, 35–36, 110
Connecticut: black governors in, 12–14
Connor, Nick, 42
Conyers, John, 32
coon: stereotype of, 18
court rulings: slavery support and, 8
Cravins, Donald, 51
crime: black constituencies and, 12
criminals: black versus white, 18
Crockett, George, 23
Curtis, Israel, 51

de facto legitimacy, 24
Dellums, Ron, 20
Delpit, Joseph, 42–43
Democratic Caucus, 35; average cohesion in, 113
Democratic Party, 2, 34, 38, 47, 67, 68, 110, 114, 115, 126, 133
Democratic Select Committee, 35–36
demographics: policy gains through, 26; voting behavior and, 12
deracialization: defined, 21
descriptive representation: defined, 23
Deukmejian, George, 19
Diggs, Charles, 35, 36

Dorsey, Yvonne, 51
Douglass, Frederick, 8, 31, 32
Dred Scott v. Sandford, 8
Dubuclet, Antoine, 41
Dukakis, Michael, 13
Duplessis, Ann, 51

Edelman, Murray, 19
Edwards, Edwin, 42
Ellickson, Mark C., 89
Emancipation Proclamation, 39
Emerson, John, 8
Entman, Robert M., 18
Epstein, David, 26–27
"Exploring the Racial Divide" (Kinder and Winter), 55

Farrakhan, Louis, 53
Fenno, Richard, 25–26
Fields, Cleo, 51, 70
Fifteenth Amendment, 9–10
Fiske, Susan, 16
Florida: former slaves in, 9
Fourteenth Amendment, 9–10
Freedom Now Party, 33, 43
From Protest to Politics (Tate), 55

Gallot, Richard, 51
Gamble, Kathleen, 142
Garnet, Henry Highland, 31
Georgia: black elected officials in, 11; former slaves in, 9
Georgia Legislative Black Caucus, 37
Gile, Roxanne, 110
Gray, William, III, 23
Grose, Christian, 27
Guinier, Lani, 90

Hall, Katie, 20
Hall v. DeCuir, 41
Hayes, Rutherford B., 41
Haynie, Kerry, 26, 48, 71, 78, 91
Hedge, David, 45, 46
Holmes, Robert, 111
Home Style (Fenno), 25–26

Index

homelessness: black constituencies and, 12
Homer Adolph Plessy v. Ferguson, 8
Honey, Avon, 51
House of Representatives, Louisiana. *See* Louisiana House of Representatives
Humphrey, Hubert, 13
Hunter, Willie, 51
Hurricane Katrina, 70, 74, 106, 109, 135–36
Hurwitz, Jon, 19

ideology, 52–53, 117–21
Illinois: black elected officials in, 11
income: black leaders and, 52–53
indentured servants: Africans as, 7; versus slavery, 8
Independents: average cohesion in, 113

Jackson, Alphonse, 43
Jackson, Jesse, 13, 19, 32, 53
Jackson, Johnny, Jr., 42–43
Jackson, Lydia P., 51
Jackson, Michael, 51
Jasper, Thomas, 42–43
Jefferson: average cohesion in, 113
Jefferson Parish, 131
Jeffries, Judson, 21
Jim Crow laws, 8–9, 10
Jindal, Bobby, 134
Johnson, Eddie Bernice, 29
Joint Center for Political and Economic Studies, 11, 13
Jones, Bryan D., 141
Jones, Charles, 51, 110
Jones, Mack H., 24
Journal of Black Studies, 111
judiciary committees: nature of, 51

Keyes, Alan, 13

LaFonta, Juan, 134
Lane v. Wilson, 10
legislation: black-interest, 74–76; estimates of passage, 98; likelihood of passing, 95–102; passage rates by group, 92, 93; success of, 95–102, 130

legislative black caucuses: emergence of, 7
Levy, Arthur, 110
Loomis, Burdett A., 35
Louisiana: black elected officials in, 11; black legislators in, 50–51; civil rights article, 40; interests in legislature, 47; legislators by education level, 49; legislators by gender, 48; legislators by party, 48; legislators by race, 49; ratification of constitution, 40. *See also* Louisiana Legislative Black Caucus
Louisiana House of Representatives: average cohesion of, 113; individual members of, 116; membership cohesion in, 114
Louisiana Legislative Black Caucus: average cohesion in, 113; black interest legislation and, 77–87; colleague relationships within, 66–69; Democratic Party and, 67–69; effectiveness of, 131–33; founding and goals of, 42–43, 130; member interviews of, 60–69; party coalitions and, 130; satellite voting and, 88–89; setting agenda for, 70–87; success rates of, 133–35; voting ideology, 130. *See also* Louisiana
Louisiana State University (LSU), 50

males: average cohesion of, 113
mammy, stereotype of, 18
Mansbridge, Jane, 23, 24
Marshall, Dale Rogers, 26
Maryland Black Caucus, 111
Massachusetts: black governors in, 12–14
McGovern, George, 13
media: stereotypes of, 17–18
Michigan: black elected officials in, 11
minority caucuses: voting cohesion in, 111–17; voting in, 109–11
minority issues, 78
Mississippi: black elected officials in, 11
Mississippi Freedom Democratic Party, 34, 43
Missouri Legislative Black Caucus, 39
Mixon, Franklin, 110
Mondale, Walter, 13

Morial, Ernest N. "Dutch," 42
Multidimensional Model of Racial Identity (MMRI), 54
Murray, Edwin, 51

NAACP. *See* National Association for the Advancement of Colored People (NAACP)
Nash, Charles E., 41
National Association for the Advancement of Colored People (NAACP), 34, 44; founding of, 10
National Black Caucus of State Legislators, 38
National Negro Convention, 30, 31
New Orleans: representatives of, 101–102, 108
New Orleans City Council, 42
New Orleans Juvenile Court, 42
newspapers: first black, 31. *See also* Douglass, Frederick
Nixon, Richard, 36
nonparty caucuses, 35
North Carolina: black elected officials in, 11
North Star, 31

O'Halloran, Sharyn, 27
Obama, Barack, 13, 14, 21, 28, 37, 53, 136; 2008 victory of, 7
Oden, Roger, 21
Orey, Byron, 91
Orleans Caucus, 95–102

Parent, Wayne, 46, 47
Participation in America (Verba and Nie), 55
Paterson, David, 12
Patrick, Deval, 12
Payne, Donald, 24
Peace and Freedom Party, 33, 43
Pease, Jane, 32
Pease, William, 32
Peffley, Mark, 19
Pierre, Wilfred, 51
Pinchback, Pinckney Benton Stewart, 40
Pinney, Neil, 110
Pohlman, Marcus, 110

Policy Agendas Project, 141
poverty: black constituencies and, 12
Powell, Colin, 53
protest organizations, 34

Quezaire, Roy, 51

racial stereotyping, 16
Reconstruction: end of, 10, 41; newly freed slaves and, 9–10
Reconstruction Act of 1867, 9–10
Redd, Marie, 23
redistricting, 13
reelection: goal of, 89–91
Republican Conference, 35
Republicans, 2, 47, 68, 71, 73, 77, 88, 91, 92, 93, 94, 95, 96, 97, 99, 100, 101, 102, 103, 107, 108, 109, 112, 113, 116, 118, 119–24
Ressler, Rand, 110
Revels, Hiram Rhodes, 10
Rhode Island: black governors in, 12–14
Rice, Condoleezza, 53
Rice, Stewart, 112
Rojecki, Andrew, 18
roll-call voting: by group, 118–20; substantive representation and, 27
Rowley, Stephanie, 54
Rural Caucus: average cohesion in, 113

Schexnider, Alvin, 22
Scott, Dred, 8
Sellers, Robert, 54
Serra, George, 110
Shelton, Nicole, 54
sickle-cell anemia, 65
slavery: economic justification for, 8; legalization of, 8; versus indentured servants, 8. *See also* Emancipation Proclamation
Smith, Mia, 54
Smith, Robert, C., 33
Smith v. Allwright, 10
social stereotypes, 17
South Carolina: 1970 governor's race, 34; black elected officials in, 11; redistricting in, 27

Index

South Carolina House of Representatives: black elected officials in, 10
South Carolina Legislative Black Caucus, 39, 44
Southern Christian Leadership Conference (SCLC), 34
Southern Democrats: ideology of, 47
Spitzer, Eliot, 12
stereotypes: as negative or positive, 17; formation of, 17–18; origin of, 16; voting behavior and, 20
Stokes, Carl A., 36
Stoudinger, Susan, 110
substantive representation, 25; roll-call voting and, 27
success rates: factors affecting, 133–35
Supreme Court: slavery support and, 8
Swain, Carol, 20, 26, 110

Tabb, David, 26
Tate, Katherine, 25
Taylor, Dorothy Mae, 42
Taylor, Shelley, 16
Texas: black elected officials in, 11
Thirteenth Amendment, 9–10
Thomas, Clarence, 53
Tom: stereotype of, 18
Turnley, Richard, Jr., 43
Tyranny of the Majority, The (Guinier), 90

unemployment: black constituencies and, 12
United Citizens Party (UCP), 34, 44
Urban League, 34, 44
U.S. Constitution: slavery support and, 8
U.S. Supreme Court: slavery support and, 8; treatment of blacks and, 41

vertical communication: defined, 24
Virginia Association of Black Elected Officials, 37
Virginia Black Caucus, 37
voter loyalty: blacks and, 26
voting behavior, 12–13
voting coalitions, 121–28
voting cohesion, 111–17
Voting Rights Act (VRA), 11, 12, 14, 28, 37, 42

Waters, Maxine, 53
Watt, Mel, 53
ways and means committees: nature of, 51
Wheat, Alan, 20
white Democrats: average cohesion among, 113
Wilder, L. Douglas, 12, 21, 22
Wilkerson, John, 141
Women: legislation introduced by, 90–91
Women's Caucus: average cohesion in, 113

Yatrakis, Kathryn, 26